Land and Agrarian Transformation in Zimbabwe

Anthem Environment and Sustainability Initiative

The Anthem Environment and Sustainability Initiative (AESI) seeks to push the frontiers of scholarship while simultaneously offering prescriptive and programmatic advice to policymakers and practitioners around the world. The programme publishes research monographs, professional and major reference works, upper-level textbooks and general interest titles. Professor Lawrence Susskind, as general editor of AESI, oversees the below book series, each with its own series editor and an editorial board featuring scholars, practitioners and business experts keen to link theory and practice.

Strategies for Sustainable Development Series

Series Editor: Professor Lawrence Susskind (MIT)
Climate Change Science, Policy and Implementation

Series Editor: Dr Brooke Hemming (US EPA)
Science Diplomacy: Managing Food, Energy and Water Sustainably

Series Editor: Professor Shafiqul Islam (Tufts University)
International Environmental Policy Series

Series Editor: Professor Saleem Ali (University of Delaware)
Big Data and Sustainable Cities Series

Series Editor: Professor Sarah Williams (MIT)
Climate Change and the Future of the North American City

Series Editor: Richardson Dilworth
(Center for Public Policy, Drexel University, United States)

Included within the AESI is the Anthem EnviroExperts Review. Through this online micro-review site, Anthem Press seeks to build a community of practice involving scientists, policy analysts and activists committed to creating a clearer and deeper understanding of how ecological systems – at every level – operate, and how they have been damaged by unsustainable development. This site publishes short reviews of important books or reports in the environmental field, broadly defined. Visit the website: www.anthemenviroexperts.com.

Land and Agrarian Transformation in Zimbabwe

Rethinking Rural Livelihoods in the Aftermath of the Land Reforms

Grasian Mkodzongi

ANTHEM PRESS

Anthem Press
An imprint of Wimbledon Publishing Company
www.anthempress.com

This edition first published in UK and USA 2022
by ANTHEM PRESS
75–76 Blackfriars Road, London SE1 8HA, UK
or PO Box 9779, London SW19 7ZG, UK
and
244 Madison Ave #116, New York, NY 10016, USA

First published in the UK and USA by Anthem Press in 2020

Copyright © Grasian Mkodzongi 2022

The author asserts the moral right to be identified as the author of this work.

British Library Cataloguing-in-Publication Data
A catalogue record for this book is available from the British Library.

Library of Congress Control Number: 2020936289

ISBN-13: 978-1-83998-575-1 (Pbk)
ISBN-10: 1-83998-575-5 (Pbk)

This title is also available as an e-book.

CONTENTS

ACKNOWLEDGEMENTS

This book would not have been possible without the involvement of a large number of people whom I cannot all mention by name. My colleagues at the University of Edinburgh were instrumental in the early stages of my doctoral research; Professor Alan Barnard, Dr Sara Dorman, Dr Joost Fontein, Dr Maggie Dwyer, Dr Joseph Mujere and others contributed to my thinking. Other colleagues such as Ian Scoones, whose work on the dynamics of livelihoods after Zimbabwe's land reforms influenced my thinking during the early stages of my research, also deserve special mention.

In Zimbabwe, Dr Ibbo Mandaza at SAPES Trust contributed to my research by allowing me to use their library facilities during fieldwork in the country. I am highly honoured to have been mentored by the late Professor Sam Moyo of the African Institute for Agrarian Studies (AIAS) who fundamentally shaped my thinking on the agrarian question in Zimbabwe. His influence continues to inspire and influence my thinking with regards to issues of agrarian transformation in Africa. Other colleagues at AIAS such as Ndabayezinhe Nyoni contributed significantly to my thinking during the formative years of my PhD research. My fieldwork assistants, Simbarashe and Tichaona Mhuriro, played an important role during the data gathering process; their support is highly appreciated.

Last, my wife Rumbi Mkodzongi and my children Yotanka, Tatanka, Ntombifuti and Prince John have significantly contributed to my work by allowing me to temporarily abandon them in pursuit of my writing.

ABBREVIATIONS

AGRITEX	Agricultural Technical and Extension Services
AIDS	Acquired Immunodeficiency Syndrome
AREX	Agricultural Rural Extension Services
ART	Anti-Retroviral Treatment
CA	Communal Areas
DA	District Administrator
DCC	District Coordinating Committees
DDC	Damvuri Development Association
DLC	District Lands Committee
FTLRP	Fast Track Land Reform Program
GNU	Government of National Unity
GoZ	Government of Zimbabwe
HIV	Human Immunodeficiency Virus
LSCF	Large-Scale Commercial Farms
MDC	Movement for Democratic Change
MLRR	Ministry of Lands and Rural Resettlement
MP	Member of Parliament
NGO	Non-Governmental Organization
NRAs	Newly Resettled Areas
RDC	Rural District Council
VIDCO	Village Development Committee
WADCO	Ward Development Committee
ZANU-PF	Zimbabwe African National Union-Patriotic Front
ZFU	Zimbabwe Farmers Union
ZIMPLATS	Zimbabwe Platinum Mines
ZNLWA	Zimbabwe National Liberation War Veterans Association

Chapter 1

INTRODUCTION: AN OVERVIEW OF ZIMBABWE'S LAND REFORM PROGRAM, 2000–20

Introduction

This book explores the outcomes of Zimbabwe's Fast Track Land Reform Program (FTLRP) which commenced in 2000. It pays particular attention to the changing dynamics of rural livelihoods occasioned by the land reform. The book is a result of a doctoral thesis submitted to the University of Edinburgh in 2013 and follow-up fieldwork as part of ongoing research on the interface of land and agrarian reform, extractives and rural livelihoods in Mhondoro Ngezi in central Zimbabwe. Since 2010 when fieldwork for the data utilized in this book was undertaken, there have been many developments in Zimbabwe which need to be captured in order to provide a more recent picture of the outcomes of Zimbabwe's FTLRP. A major development which took place recently was the ouster of Zimbabwe's late former president, Robert Mugabe, by a military-assisted coup in late 2017. While his removal was celebrated by the majority of Zimbabweans, such celebrations seem to have been 'too early' as the economic situation has worsened under the leadership of Emmerson Mnangagwa. The situation is characterized by the widespread shortage of fuel and frequent electricity outages which have crippled industry, leading many people to question the leadership of Emmerson Mnangagwa and his so-called new dispensation.

The dramatic removal of Robert Mugabe has ushered in a new trajectory in the politics of land. Zimbabwe's newly elected president, Mnangagwa, has sought to distance himself from Mugabe's radical policies in favour of appeasing Western countries which had imposed sanctions on Zimbabwe in response to the seizure and redistribution of white-owned farmlands. Since assuming power after the harmonized elections of July 2018, Mnangagwa has reversed many Mugabe-era policies such as the indigenization and local empowerment regulations which, among other things, compelled foreign-owned companies to give a 51 per cent controlling stake to indigenous Zimbabweans. These policies were viewed by Western countries as antagonistic to foreign direct investment (FDI). Furthermore, the new government has adopted a more liberal agrarian policy, with promises to compensate former white farmers who lost their land during the implementation of the fast track land reforms in 2000. In addition, the new government has also promised to undertake a land audit in order to address distortions in the land ownership structure. The land audit is anticipated to address land conflicts and land tenure security issues which are believed to be hampering agrarian investments especially in the A2 commercial farm sector.

Under the 'Zimbabwe is open for business' mantra, foreign capitalists have been encouraged to come and invest in Zimbabwe's key economic sectors such as agriculture and mining. The push to liberalize the economy has led to the abandonment of the heterodox macroeconomic framework popularized during the Mugabe era. It is anticipated that embracing neoliberalism will lead to the removal of sanctions and an increase in FDIs. These sanctions have undermined Zimbabwe's ability to borrow money from international finance institutions such as the World Bank and International Monetary Fund to kick-start the economy.

While Mnangagwa's pro-Western rhetoric has been applauded in Western capitals for the dramatic shift in policy in favour of neoliberal orthodoxy, there has not been any meaningful financial rewards for his appeal to normalize relations with Western countries. Instead, the US government has further renewed sanctions on Zimbabwe with demands for democratic reforms before sanctions can be reversed. The inability of Western countries to respond to Mnangagwa's reconciliatory tone by removing sanctions and providing the much-needed capital to rebuild the economy has left many Zimbabweans wondering if the re-engagement policy will address the many economic challenges facing the country.

Since Mnangagwa assumed office after a contested electoral outcome, the socio-economic situation in Zimbabwe has worsened. Fuel shortages and electricity cuts have resurfaced due to foreign currency shortages. In addition, cash shortages and rising exchange rates between the US dollar and the local currency (the recently reintroduced Zimbabwe dollar) have further pushed the prices of basic commodities towards an upward trajectory. As a result, the price of farm inputs such as seed and fertilizer has also shot up, leaving many farmers unable to afford them and hence adequately prepare for the planting season. Thus, Mnangagwa's hasty move to embrace neoliberalism wholesale poses major challenges for Zimbabwe's fledgling agrarian sector. With a stagnated economy, promises to compensate former white farmers seem to be problematic when the country cannot afford fuel, electricity and other critical imports.

Moreover, promises for a return to land markets are likely to reconfigure the new agrarian structure in favour of large-scale agribusinesses to the detriment of peasants and small-scale capitalist producers who had so far dominated

the agricultural sector after the land reform. There are indications that foreign capitalists are lining up to re-enter Zimbabwe's agrarian sector through
contract farming arrangements and joint ventures with black Zimbabweans.
The joint ventures, which are disguised as FDIs, signal a new process of primitive accumulation based on commodity production for export. This process
has intensified, especially in the tobacco sector where peasants have become
the main producers of the crop. While tobacco production has become a key
driver of accumulation from below among a socially differentiated peasantry,
it has also led to the reinsertion of peasants into global commodity circuits
under unfavourable terms.

The dramatic shift towards neoliberal orthodoxy has long-term consequen-
ces for Zimbabwe's agrarian sector. Apart from its potential to reverse a trajectory of repeasantization witnessed in Zimbabwe after the fast track land
reform, there are now fears of land grabbing and ecological destruction linked
to the financialization of agriculture and the return of large-scale farms. Under
the new political dispensation, so-called foreign investors who are acquiring
land for agricultural investments are demanding the issuance of freehold
tenures and access to cheap land and labour. This is detrimental to the interests
of peasants and other vulnerable groups who might lose their land to these
disguised forms of land grabbing. The rushed reversal of the indigenization
and empowerment regulations in favour of global mining capital is likely to fast
track the grabbing of mineral-rich lands from local populations.

While indigenization regulations had their own controversies, they acted
as a buffer against the wanton grabbing of lands and extraction of minerals
by large capitalist enterprises at the expense of local populations. Moreover,
these regulations provided guarantees that extractive companies acquired
a social licence to operate before commencing operations. The removal of
these regulations has taken away the only leverage that local communities
had over mining companies. Such companies no longer need to comply with
local empowerment regulations by investing in local communities, but can
easily bypass them with the support of government. It is increasingly clear
that the new government has chosen to pursue a neoliberal path which seeks
to reverse the agrarian transformation process in favour of so-called foreign
investors. However, the process does not enjoy political legitimacy as many
ordinary Zimbabweans view the current trajectory in favour of global capital
as a betrayal of the masses and the gains of the liberation struggle.

Zimbabwe's Fast Track Land Reform Program: An Overview

Until a decade ago, the outcomes of Zimbabwe's FTLRP initiated in 2000
were highly contested (Hammar et al. 2003; Moyo and Yeros 2005; Moyo

et al. 2009; Scoones et al. 2010; Zamchiya 2011; Hanlon et al. 2012; Matondi 2012; Mkodzongi 2013). In the period immediately after its commencement, it was claimed that the land reform had largely benefited supporters of the Zimbabwe African National Union Patriotic Front (ZANU PF) political party (Hammar et al. 2003; Zamchiya 2011). Furthermore, the land occupations which characterized the implementation of the FTLRP were simply depicted as a return to barbarism and the abuse of human rights by Zimbabwe's former president Robert Mugabe's regime (Worby 2003). Selected acts of violence during the land occupations were used to show how these occupations were not about land hunger, but a 'political gimmick' by Mugabe to entrench his dictatorial rule.

In the media-driven frenzy which followed, peasants who occupied white-owned commercial farms were depicted as environmental bandits who were more interested in natural resource extraction than farming. Google maps were used to show the dramatic ecological degradation which had taken place across Zimbabwe's former white-owned commercial farming areas as evidence of an environmental disaster triggered by the land reform (Richardson 2005). The historical injustices in the land ownership structure which had persisted post-Zimbabwe's independence were simply ignored in favour of a dominant narrative which reduced the land reform to a political gimmick.

Furthermore, the forceful eviction of white farmers was seen as having undermined Zimbabwe's agrarian-based economy. Nostalgic claims of Zimbabwe having been a 'bread basket' of Southern Africa before the evictions of white land owners, and a 'basket case' in the aftermath, became popular in the media and in academic writing. White farmers were often depicted as having been the backbone of Zimbabwe's agricultural economy, without whose skills the country could not feed itself. Furthermore, they were also depicted as de facto environmental activists whose eviction had endangered the environment. The decline in agricultural productivity witnessed after the land reform was simply reduced to the eviction of white farmers. Other contributory factors such as severe weather patterns (which are a common occurrence in Zimbabwe and the wider subregion) and the prevailing difficult socio-economic and political climate which undermined the ability of the ZANU PF government to support the new farmers were largely ignored.

A major weakness of the discourse of chaos and agricultural decline was the lack of empirical evidence. Many of the claims made in the early period have been proven to be largely misleading given new empirical evidence which has emerged post the fast track land reform (Moyo et al. 2009; Scoones et al. 2010; Chambati 2011; Moyo, S. 2011a; Hanlon et al. 2012; Matondi 2012; Mkodzongi 2013; Mutopo 2014). These studies have demonstrated that the outcomes of Zimbabwe's fast track land reform were broad, and that a nuanced analysis needs to be undertaken before broad generalizations can be made. More importantly, empirical data shows that although the land reform was underpinned by class, gender and ethno-regionalism, landless peasants were the major beneficiaries (Moyo et al. 2009; Scoones et al. 2010; Hanlon et al. 2012), and that access to new land has enhanced the livelihoods of newly resettled peasant households (Mkodzongi 2013).

Although some of the new farmers, particularly in the A2 sector (commercial farms), have struggled to utilize the land, claims that the new farmers are 'weekend' or 'cell phone' farmers have been proven to be misleading. Empirical data from across various study sites (Moyo et al. 2009; Scoones et al. 2010; Hanlon et al. 2012) shows that the new farmers, in particular the A1 sector (peasant farmers), have made relatively large investments on their newly acquired land despite a hostile socio-economic environment which has obtained after the land reform. Additionally, although the agrarian sector is yet to fully recover post the land reforms, empirical data shows that certain subsectors of agriculture have recovered, and that some of the new farmers are already 'accumulating from below' (Scoones et al. 2010). This is especially the case with tobacco where by 2013, over 91,278 farmers were registered tobacco growers.

Data from the Tobacco Industry Marketing Board (TIMB) shows that 82 per cent of the registered growers are peasant farmers (based in both communal areas and A1). This makes them the major supplier of the crop post the land reform. More importantly, by 2014, the total number of registered tobacco growers had risen to 106,456, an annual increase of almost 10 per cent (TIMB 2014). The tobacco sector contributes 10 per cent of Zimbabwe's annual GDP; the entire value chain employs more than 1.2 million people with an estimated 5 million dependents (ibid.). The fact that this sector is now dominated by peasants shows how the land reform has enhanced rural livelihoods. It is important to highlight here that the upsurge in tobacco production by peasants has engendered an exploitative labour regime whose dynamics are yet to be fully investigated. However, this is beyond the scope of this book.

It has been argued that the fast track land reform transformed a bimodal agrarian structure inherited from colonialism, and replaced it with a trimodal structure which has broadened participation in productive agriculture. According to S. Moyo (2011), the dismantling of the large farms has expanded the number of smallholders, while deracializing and diversifying the commercial agricultural sector beyond white minority producers who dominated the sector before the land reform (ibid.). This had the dual effect of freeing up excess land and bringing efficiency to the agricultural sector. More importantly, empirical data gathered in the Mhondoro Ngezi District (Mkodzongi 2013) and other areas (Scoones et al. 2010; Hanlon et al. 2012) shows that beneficiaries of the land reform now have access to better quality land and other natural resources; this has led to the diversification of livelihoods post the land reforms.

Peasants, Redistributive Land Reform and Rural Livelihoods

The peasantry as an analytical category has a long history. Competing interpretations of what 'peasants' are have influenced ongoing debates about the benefits of land reform between so-called agrarian pessimists and agrarian populists (Bryceson et al. 2000; Byres 2004; Moyo and Yeros 2005; Rosset et al. 2006; van der Ploeg 2008; Bernstein 2009). The concept of the peasant adopted here is that put forward by Boltvinik (2010: 4) who defines peasants as 'smallholders that work their land, individual plots of land as their principal source of income'. Peasants are also perceived as small farmers who largely rely on family labour for their farm production (Moyo and Yeros 2005). It is important to highlight that the concept of peasants adopted here does not denote a homogenous category. Peasants are socially differentiated; some are rich peasants and are able to invest in production and to hire labour. Others are worker peasants who generally rely on both farming and wage family labour. Some are poor peasants who do not have access to land and thus mainly rely on selling their labour power (Bernstein 2009: 431). Below is an analysis of conceptual issues that have shaped historical debates about peasants and land and agrarian reform.

It has been argued that redistributive land reform is a sine qua non for the transformation of the role of various agrarian classes in struggles for development and democratization towards equitable land ownership and social relations of production (Byres 1991, 1996). Land rights and ownership tend to grow out of power relationships. Thus, land owners have historically employed coercive methods and distortions in land, labour, credit and commodity markets to extract economic rents from land and from peasants (Bernstein 2009). Such rent-seeking behaviour reduces the efficiency of resource use, undermines growth and increases the poverty of rural populations (Binswanger et al. 1993). It has also been argued that land reform as a key dimension of agrarian reform is a necessary but insufficient condition for national development (Moyo and Yeros 2005), and is also key to agricultural and social transformation (Chang 2009). Within the postcolonial context of Southern Africa, it has been argued that 'land reform and accumulation from below are necessary to reconfigure a dualistic and unequal agrarian structure which is itself a structural cause of poverty' (Cousins 2010: 15).

In postcolonial settler economies such as those of southern Africa, the political objectives of land reform involve, inter alia, restructuring the 'distribution of land ownership towards a democratic agrarian structure to promote social, economic, and political transformation which creates security of tenure for all, through legally enforceable system of property rights which does not necessarily mean private property' (Moyo, S. 2011a: 2). Historically, agrarian elites tend to be an economically powerful and politically reactionary landed class that monopolizes land and forces most of the population into the role of landless laborers and, as such, reduces incentives among land-owners and workers to invest (Evans 2009). Where there is a history of a dual-istic agrarian structure such as in Zimbabwe and other former settler colonies (South Africa and Namibia), redistributive land reform is necessary since it transforms agrarian relations and enhances the ability of peasants to access 'ecological capital' (van der Ploeg 2010) which will enhance their social repro-duction strategies. Empirical data gathered in Mhondoro Ngezi indicate that access to land and other natural resources formerly enclosed under dualistic tenure arrangements can enhance rural livelihoods and address rural poverty. It has also been argued that within the context of globalization, access to land by small-scale farmers gives them 'food sovereignty' (Rosset et al. 2006) as it helps them to gain control over agricultural value chains rather than rely on agribusinesses for their livelihoods. Within the Zimbabwean context, various empirical studies undertaken in the aftermath of land reform (Hanlon et al. 2012; Scoones et al. 2012) and data gathered in Mhondoro Ngezi demon-strate that the breaking up of large private landholdings is a prerequisite for transforming the lives of marginalized rural households. Such a process takes away monopoly syndicates and their speculative tendencies, which undermine efficiency, productivity and equity in the agrarian sector.

The link between redistributive land reform and rural livelihoods has been a subject of an ongoing farm size debate historically linked to the classic agrarian question (Bernstein 2009). According to Scoones et al. (2010: 120), 'For agriculture pessimists, redistributive land reform based on a smallholder model makes little sense beyond temporary welfare relief unless combined with substantial investment in off-farm enterprise development with firm links to urban areas.' Agriculture pessimists such as Bryceson et al. (2000) and Ellis (2000) have challenged the benefits of smallholder farming. They have argued that the countryside is experiencing a form of 'de-agrarianization' and that small-scale agriculture can no longer provide secure livelihoods for peasant households that are forced to engage in more profitable off-farm activities rather than farming. Others such as Byres (2004) argue that redistributive land reform 'runs contrary to historical forces of capitalism' and is largely based on the historical fantasy of agrarian populists.

However, these arguments run contrary to Zimbabwe's recent experience with land reform. The Mhondoro Ngezi case and other empirical studies undertaken across the country's diverse agroecological regions (Moyo et al. 2009; Scoones et al. 2010; Hanlon et al. 2012) demonstrate that redistributive land reform can have a positive impact on the lives of peasant farmers by allowing them access to land and natural resources which have been enclosed and enjoyed by a few whites under the bimodal agrarian structure inherited from colonialism. Additionally, such studies have indicated that smallholder farmers have the capability to utilize the land and take advantage of domestic markets and value chains associated with land reform (Scoones et al. 2010; Moyo, S. 2011a). The dramatic growth of the tobacco sector which is now dominated by peasants testifies to the above.

It has further been argued by so-called agrarian populists that although large commercial farms can be more productive, they tend to suffer from productivity inefficiencies because they require large amounts of capital and labour to operate, whereas family-run smallholder farms are more efficient (although this does not mean they are more productive) and cheaper to run since they employ family labour (Binswanger et al. 1993). This argument is based on the fact that the reduction in transaction costs, especially over the supervision of farm labour associated with small-scale family farming, results in higher returns than large-scale capitalist farming (Berry and Cline 1979).

This book utilizes empirical data gathered over a period of 10 years with peasant households in central Zimbabwe to demonstrate that redistributive land reform can have a positive impact on the lives of historically marginalized rural populations. For example, in Mhondoro Ngezi District in Mashonaland West Province, land reform has allowed landless peasants to access better-quality land and other natural resources which they could not access under the previous agrarian structure. Ownership of land 'represents autonomy and opportunity to create a livelihood' (van der Ploeg 2010: 3). Therefore, land reform has provided an opportunity for peasant households to socially reproduce themselves on diverse livelihood portfolios and is likely to have a positive impact on their lives in the long term. For example, after the land reforms, peasants can now straddle livelihoods across diverse activities such as artisanal gold mining (Mkodzongi and Spiegel 2018) and other wider natural resource extraction activities, given the fact that agriculture alone cannot sustain them. This was not possible under the previous agrarian structure as most agroecologically rich lands were enclosed and natural resources were enjoyed by a few whites.

Although the new farmers have faced a difficult socio-economic environment after resettlement which has hindered agricultural investments, they have made relatively large investments, especially in the case of A1 farmers who, against all odds, have taken advantage of the new land to improve their lives. Moreover, those who have struggled to utilize the newly acquired land are involved in a wide variety of activities which generate capital critical for future agricultural investments. While recurrent droughts and lack of state support due to an ongoing economic crisis have undermined agricultural productivity, the resilience of the smallholder farmers against many odds stacked against them must be highlighted. The massive productivity witnessed in the tobacco sector where peasants have become the major producers of the crop indicates that when peasants are given land and technical support, they can improve production.

Furthermore, tobacco production has boosted both rural and urban economies by creating employment and markets for urban-based businesses that sell their machinery, furniture and agricultural inputs to the tobacco farmers. It is also important to highlight here that tobacco production has also helped to reinsert peasants into commodity markets under unfavourable terms. While contract farming arrangements which are now dominating tobacco production among the peasantry have been an important source of capital for agricultural investments, they have also deepened exploitative labour relations and pushed some farmers into debt after failing to pay back money advanced to them in form of agricultural inputs. Tobacco contract farming has also pushed the risks of agricultural production to the peasant farmers who are left in debt in the event of climate-induced droughts and crop failure. The dynamics underpinning tobacco production thus point to a new wave of primitive accumulation of capital that is currently unfolding in the tobacco sector. Its long-term dynamics require further research beyond the scope of this book.

Data Gathering in Mhondoro Ngezi

The data utilized in this book was initially gathered in 2010 at a time when the political process in Zimbabwe had stabilized after nearly a decade of socio-economic decline, contested electoral processes and political violence. During the time, debates on the outcomes of Zimbabwe's FTLRP were being largely driven by claims and counterclaims based on very thin evidence. However, the onset of the Government of National Unity (GNU) in 2009 after a contested electoral process heralded a period of relative political stability in Zimbabwe. This meant that going to the study site was relatively safer than before when the political situation was very tense. Moreover, life became relatively easier after the 'dollarization' of the economy, although the situation has worsened economically as highlighted earlier.

However, the changes in the socio-economic and political environment and the relative ease with which one could access the fieldwork site did not make data gathering as easy as I expected. To start with, any research focusing on the dynamics of land reform in Zimbabwe was likely to encounter some challenges given the emotive and political nature of land in the country. Newly resettled areas were highly politicized during land occupations and, as a result, resettled farmers were highly suspicious of outsiders wanting to ask questions about land. Such outsiders were generally viewed as a security threat as people were never sure if one was a spy or a supporter of opposition political parties. The proliferation of authority structures in the countryside all exercising some form of authority over land meant that getting the clearance to access research informants was a daunting task. Fast track land reform reconfigured rural authority structures, despite being already a multi-layered authority structure; new authority structures, such as seven member committees, ZANU PF District Coordinating Committees (DCCs) and war veterans, were added. Thus, securing a clearance to undertake fieldwork was a rather complicated process which was also time-consuming. To make matters even more challenging, these authority structures were riddled with factionalism, ethno-regionalism and competed to demonstrate their authority. This meant that being given clearance by one authority, such as, for example, a local MP or chief, did not necessarily guarantee you unfettered access to research informants as other authorities could simply block you.

The main challenge was the absence of a clear hierarchical structure which could govern how such structures function as there is often discord and competition between them. For example, my field assistant and I interviewed people in six villages out of the total eight we intended to interview; and when we arrived in village seven, a war veteran threatened to confiscate our data and asked us to go to seek clearance from the councillor. It was after a long negotiation that he finally allowed us to proceed. This prolonged process of negotiating with a diversity of authority structures was both time-consuming and financially expensive as it meant a longer period in the study site.

Another challenge I faced was that chiefs from the nearby Mhondoro Ngezi Communal Area who had made territorial claims over the newly resettled area (where the research site is located) were not resident in these areas, although they exercised some form of authority through their proxies who are resident in the new areas. A clearance from all the three chiefs had to be secured before interviews could be undertaken. This further delayed the data gathering process and also added more expenses to an already overstretched research budget.

In addition, in the early stages of the data gathering process, people in newly resettled areas were reluctant to discuss land issues with a stranger. Authority structures, in particular ZANU PF, were against strangers asking about land reform for fear that such people wanted to undermine the credibility of the land reform process. The main cause of this was that some academics had undertaken research which portrayed the outcomes of land reform negatively.

Such research was blamed for being central to the way Western countries adjusted their foreign policy towards Zimbabwe, and in particular the imposition of targeted sanctions. As a result, ZANU PF officials were suspicious of any academic researchers with links to Western universities who were suspected of undermining Zimbabwe's image abroad. Research informants were therefore very suspicious in the beginning despite the fact that clearance from higher authorities was there and that I was a local student. People were afraid that they might give out information that would portray land reform negatively and thus attract the attention of authorities. Since there was a general perception that security of tenure was associated with supporting ZANU PF, many people feared that interviews might leave them vulnerable to losing their land after being suspected of colluding with foreign interests. This left me facing ethical dilemmas as I did not want to expose informants to political victimization. As a result, it took me longer than expected to establish some rapport before being acknowledged in the villages.

There were also other problems associated with my positionality as a local researcher from a foreign university. One might have thought being a Zimbabwean would have made the job of data gathering easier. However, due to local political dynamics, it turned out that my Zimbabwean identity actually worked against me. I did not expect that my presence in the community would threaten some local politicians. For example, some local political leaders suspected that my research might be a form of information gathering which I would use in the long term to campaign in local future parliamentary elections. My activities and social interactions with research informants initially raised a lot of suspicion.

My research assistant also further complicated the situation by mistakenly telling my potential informants that I was doing the research to identify the challenges faced by farmers and that I was going to link them with donors. This seemed like a typical political campaign strategy which threatened local politicians. This resulted in me being asked to address a village meeting discussing 'development' at which I was the 'keynote' speaker tasked with providing information about where the farmers could get financial resources and other technical support to address local challenges such as shortage of clean water, construction of schools, HIV/AIDS, and so on. I had to spend more time explaining to the local leadership that I was not linked to any donor and that I was a researcher interested in knowing what the new farmers were doing with land and what new opportunities were available to them in terms of livelihoods; where they came from and how they came and what they thought about their new environment. The local leadership had to be convinced that there were no political ambitions and that instead I was only interested in the outcomes of land reform rather than contesting local political positions.

After addressing the suspicions and misinformation about my research in the area, it became relatively easy to spend time with many farmers from all eight villages at the former Damvuri Conservancy and to arrange interviews with key informants such as AREX officers, chiefs, representatives of the Committee of Seven, Village Development Committees (VIDCOs), Ward Development Committees (WADCOs), war veterans, headmen and the local ZANU PF leadership.

Gathering data had its own pitfalls which are explained below. For example, initial interviews were with local war veterans due to the fact that they were responsible for organizing the occupation of the Damvuri Conservancy. In the initial interviews, these war veterans posited a narrative that was common across Zimbabwe at the time that they had taken the Damvuri Conservancy through *jambanja* (use of violence) – and had forcibly evicted the former white owner, Owain Lewis, and given the land to the people. However, during my stay in the villages, a more nuanced story gradually began to emerge which contradicted what had generally looked like the 'official' version of what happened during the occupation of Damvuri.

Contrary to war veterans claims of *jambanja* style of land occupations, many of the informants enunciated that the Damvuri Conservancy had been resettled relatively peacefully with no *jambanja* at all. According to this 'alternative' narrative which was corroborated by many informants, when the war veterans arrived and occupied the conservancy, the owner approached the district administrator (DA) in the nearby Kadoma town and requested a grace period in order for him to pack his property and vacate the land. It was also learnt that the DA agreed to the land owner's proposal and advised the war veterans not to interfere with the farmer's property and to guard against any criminal activities such as hunting and cutting the game perimeter fence until the former owner had vacated the land. The owner was even allowed to take some of the wild animals with him.

This story was very difficult for an outsider to comprehend given the fact that war veterans and local ZANU PF activists who are the community gatekeepers seemed to have their own 'official' version of the story of how the land was occupied and redistributed. This had something to do with local dynamics of authority after land reform. War veterans sought to project themselves as 'liberators of the land' in an attempt to justify their claims of authority over land. However, this had the effect of projecting a problematic narrative of what actually happened during the occupation. My experience at Damvuri is that the war veteran identity is problematic in terms of their role in land occupations and the way undue agency is sometimes attributed to them in some places by some scholars (Sadomba 2008).

Another challenge that emerged during the data gathering process was the issue of gender. Interviewing women proved to be a rather difficult process as it involved in some places negotiating with their husbands before clearance was granted. In one instance, data that had been gathered after interviewing a woman was confiscated by the husband, who claimed that women knew nothing about land reform and that if we wanted to know anything about land reform, we had to interview him instead. Although there are a relatively big number of women who accessed land in their own right in Mhondoro Ngezi, women continue to play a subordinate role in agricultural issues after land reform, especially married women. However, their husbands did not readily allow the researcher access to interview them. This made it more difficult to gather women's perspectives compared to those of the men. However, a relatively large number of women were interviewed after negotiating with their husbands.

My interaction with research informants from diverse backgrounds and of both genders helped me to develop a deeper understanding of the dynamics that shaped the way the land occupations unfolded in Mhondoro Ngezi. This helped me to trace the life histories of the informants, some of whom had been forcibly evicted from the area in the 1950s and had come back through land reform. These histories were central to the way many people made claims over land. Spending time resident in the villages helped me to develop closer relationships with the informants and to improve my understanding of their life histories and how such histories had shaped their livelihoods. It also helped me to understand the broader meanings attached to land and how the farmers conceptualized the benefits of land reform. My social interactions and personal relationships with informants improved my understanding of how land reform had shaped rural livelihoods and also helped to illuminate the centrality of land restitution in the way people made claims over land.

A large corpus of the data utilized in this book is based on ethnographic data gathered through structured and semi-structured interviews, focus group discussions, informal conversations and personal observations. In order to complement the qualitative data, a baseline survey of 50 households was also undertaken as a way of tracing changes in ownership of property such as livestock and farm equipment which had occurred after resettlement. This was useful in highlighting how livelihoods had changed after the land reform.

Secondary sources have also been utilized to provide a background to the debate on land reform in Zimbabwe. Such sources were useful in highlighting major debates that had emerged in the aftermath of land reform. They were also useful in highlighting the outcomes of land reform in other parts of Zimbabwe and hence helped to refine the book.

Last, some archival work was undertaken in order to provide a historical background to the Mhondoro Ngezi area, in particular the dynamics of forced removals in the former Rhodesdale Estate, which became salient in the context of land reform. Moreover, archival sources, in particular Native Commissioner Delineation Reports, were useful in highlighting the background of the three chieftainships (Benhura, Nyika and Murambwa) that have made territorial claims in the newly resettled areas (NRAs) in Mhondoro Ngezi District. These reports were particularly useful in highlighting the genealogy of the chieftaincies and the dynamics of boundaries between their territories starting from the colonial era to the 2000s when such boundaries became contested. It is hoped that this combination of data gathering methods, and the use of secondary materials, improves the quality of the data, and more importantly the objectivity of the book's findings.

Although this book is based on a case study of 185 households in one district, it is hoped that its findings can be generalized to other parts of Zimbabwe. It is also hoped that the book will add to the growing number of studies focusing on the outcomes of Zimbabwe's fast track land reforms, and in particular the new trajectory of livelihoods occasioned by a change in agrarian structure (Moyo et al. 2009; Scoones et al. 2010; Hanlon et al. 2012; Matondi 2012; Mutopo 2014).

Since the initial data gathering in 2010, follow-on field work has been undertaken and the field work site extended to accommodate new research interests. The changes in the political environment, especially the removal of former president Robert Mugabe in 2017, has led to a more tolerant political environment which allowed a more in-depth data gathering process without fear of political violence. There is thus less paranoia and fear among research informants as was the case when I initially undertook field work in 2010 when the political atmosphere was tense. This has not only made the research site more accessible but significantly improved the quality of the data that could be gathered as people are now more open than they were a decade ago.

Structure of the Book

This book provides an analysis of the dynamics of the land reform process in central Zimbabwe by utilizing the life histories of people who were resettled at the Damvuri Conservancy in Mhondoro Ngezi in Mashonaland West Province. The book tells a detailed story about how the land reform unfolded, the political dynamics that underpinned it, social organization of the newly resettled farmers and the new trajectory of livelihoods occasioned by the land reform. As a result, the chapters in the book highlight the dynamics of land reform in the Mhondoro Ngezi District as highlighted below. Due to the recent political developments in Zimbabwe, the trajectory of livelihoods among farmers is changing, especially given the economic challenges facing the country. As noted earlier, the return to neoliberalism under the new government is likely to have a negative impact on the livelihoods of peasants who benefited from the land reform. More importantly, the return to neoliberal land markets might unravel the new agrarian structure which until recently was favourable to peasants. The new joint venture arrangements between foreign investors and black capitalists in the agricultural and mining sectors signify the grabbing of land and natural resources which might undermine the livelihoods of rural populations in the long term.

Chapter 1 analyses major debates that have emerged in the aftermath of land reform through a review of literature. It also sets out the focus of the book and its contribution to the broader debates on literature on the outcomes of Zimbabwe's land reform process. In addition, it also highlights how the political changes that have recently taken place in Zimbabwe are likely to affect various agrarian classes, in particular the peasantry.

Chapter 2 provides an analysis of the dynamics that influenced the way the fast track land reform unfolded in the Mhondoro Ngezi District. It pays particular attention on how people were mobilized, the logistics involved in joining land occupations and the political dynamics that underpinned such a process. The chapter challenges some of the generalizations popularized in literature, especially the role of war veterans, customary authorities and the state, in the way land occupations unfolded across the Zimbabwean countryside.

Chapter 3 provides a biographical sketch of the beneficiaries in terms of their places of origin, ownership of assets and the logistics and socio-economic dynamics that influenced the way they made claims over land in Mhondoro Ngezi. The chapter shows how historical grievances over 'ancestral' lands influenced the way people made claims over land. As a result, discourses of 'autochthony and belonging' became salient during the land occupations and in the aftermath.

Chapter 4 highlights the reconfiguration of rural authority structures during the implementation of the FTLRP. It shows how during the land reform, war veterans and chiefs became prominent political actors in the countryside with authority over land. This created a multitiered structure of authority which led to the temporary 'suspension bureaucracy' in the countryside, a development which challenged the hegemonic role of the state in the countryside. The chapter shows how in the aftermath of the land reform, authority over the newly resettled land is contested between customary authorities and the state, although the later has sought to reclaim a hegemonic role in the countryside post the land reforms.

Chapter 5 analyses the trajectory of livelihoods post the land reforms. The chapter shows how the land reform has allowed newly resettled farmers access to better-quality land and other natural resources which were previously enclosed and enjoyed by a few whites under the previous agrarian structure. The chapter argues that although land remains central to the way peasant households socially reproduce themselves, livelihoods are now diversified due to improved mobility and new livelihood opportunities opened up by the land reform.

Chapter 6 explores the dynamics of social organization post the land reforms. In particular, it shows how after the land reforms, new kinship ties and social organizations have emerged. These new social structures play a key role in the way people are socially organized given the fact that many people came from diverse geographical and ethnic backgrounds which led to conflicts, especially in the earlier period. The chapter also shows how the absence of social services in the newly resettled areas forced people to initiate new associational networks in order to address the many challenges they faced post the land reform.

Chapter 7 provides a summary of the key findings of the book, in particular how the land reform has ushered in a new trajectory of livelihoods across Zimbabwe's countryside. It also highlights some aspects of the new agrarian structure which remain unresolved and thus require further research. This is especially the case with multiple farm ownership, informal land markets, land tenure and conflicts over land which are likely to be a source of future struggles over land. Given the recent political developments in the country, this concluding chapter highlights future agrarian scenarios within the context of a neoliberal macroeconomic framework which was recently adopted by the Mnangagwa government. The potential impact of the new policy trajectory, especially on the peasantry, is also highlighted.

Chapter 2

RECLAIMING THE LAND IN MHONDORO NGEZI

In Mhondoro Ngezi, land occupations started in earnest as symbolic manoeuvres by war veterans protesting against local grievances of rural poverty and landlessness during the so-called *jambanja* era (Chaumba et al. 2003). The first core group of the war veterans arrived at the Damvuri conservancy in 2000 led by two war veteran leaders, Comrade (Cde) Jongwe and Cde Hunidzananaiwa. Cde Jongwe came from the Bandawe old resettlement area near the Damvuri conservancy while Cde Hunidzananaiwa is believed to have come from Sanyati. They both belonged to the local Kadoma chapter of the Zimbabwe National Liberation and War Veterans Association (ZNLWVA). The war veterans were later joined by people from the old resettlement schemes bordering the Damvuri conservancy and also by residents of the nearby Mhondoro Ngezi Communal Area (CA) and others from areas further away such as Sanyati and Gokwe.

An important dynamic of land occupations in Mhondoro Ngezi which is worth noting is that they did not follow the popularized *jambanja* style, which in some places involved violent confrontation between war veteran-led peasants and the white land owners during the watershed moments of 2000 (Hammar et al. 2003). Instead, these land occupations were relatively peaceful and the war veterans who occupied the conservancy were forced to observe law and order before the conservancy was officially demarcated into A1 plots. The reason for the absence of *jambanja* can be attributed to the fact that the district administrator (DA) in Kadoma was involved at the early stages of the occupation. The DA is believed to have been approached by the owner of the Damvuri conservancy who requested time to move his property from the occupied land before it was distributed. Thus, the DA is said to have ordered war veterans not to interfere with the farmer's property.

The way land seekers came to the occupied conservancy is another important dynamic of the Damvuri land occupations. Although a few people joined the war veterans who had camped at the conservancy in 2000, a large number of people who were officially allocated plots had formally registered with the DA in Kadoma before moving to the conservancy. Most land seekers from far off areas such as Gokwe did not join the occupation but camped first at the DA's office where they were 'processed' before being transported to the occupied conservancy. However, there were other people who came through ZANU PF networks within the Mashonaland West Province. Some people who came from as far as Harare and other cities and towns were also allocated land at the Damvuri conservancy at a later stage. This indicates that land occupations at Damvuri conservancy were an ordered process from the beginning and that war veterans had limited authority to redistribute land. Yet another dynamic of the land occupations in Mhondoro Ngezi is that a large number of people who were resettled at the conservancy claimed an autochthonous connection with the area. Such people claimed that they had been forcefully removed from the area during the colonial era and relocated to the nearby Mhondoro Ngezi CA or to remote areas of Gokwe. For such people fast track land reform provided an opportunity to recover their ancestral lands lost during the colonial era.

The way in which the conservancy was occupied in terms of the dominance of bureaucratic processes rather than *jambanja* had a significant influence on how the newly occupied land was governed in the aftermath of the land reform process. The following section provides a historical background to the Mhondoro Ngezi area.

Historical Background to the Damvuri Conservancy

The Damvuri conservancy is located in the former large-scale commercial farming (LSCF) area of the Mhondoro Ngezi District in Mashonaland West Province of Zimbabwe. The area where the conservancy is located was historically part of a large stretch of land called Rhodesdale Estate which bordered the mining town of Mvuma to the east and the towns of Kadoma, Kwekwe and Gweru to the west. The estate had a chequered history; it changed hands from being part of the vast landholdings owned by the British South Africa Company (BSAC) when it was acquired by the London Rhodesia Corporation (LONRHO) and then sold to the Rhodesian government in the late 1940s. Rhodesdale was acquired by the Rhodesian government in the 1940s in order to provide land to British veterans of World War II who had emigrated to the then Southern Rhodesia (Nyambara 2005).

The sale of Rhodesdale to the Rhodesian government and its subsequent demarcation into private farms resulted in the eviction of Africans who had been allowed to live on the estate as tenant farmers, paying rent to the BSAC during the early days of colonial occupation. During this time, it was generally profitable for European land owners to collect rent as farming was not

viable. However, the situation changed with time and the post-war agricultural boom led to a high demand for Rhodesian agricultural products and
hence a demand for more land for European use. Moreover, an increase in net
emigration to Rhodesia by Europeans further increased the demand for land
to resettle such immigrants. This led to what has been generally called the
'second alienation' (Ranger 1985). During this time large numbers of Africans,
who despite the requirements of the Land Apportionment Act which specified
that they relocate had remained on European areas as tenant farmers, faced
forceful evictions. Under the context of the post-war dynamics which led to
increased demand for land, an amendment was made to laws that had allowed
the Africans to continue living on European areas as 'tenants' turned them to
being 'squatters', legitimizing forceful removal to 'native' areas.

Most of the Africans evicted from Rhodesdale were forcibly relocated to
native reserves in Sanyati and the largely uninhabited Gokwe areas. Before
their evictions, such Africans had been successful tenant farmers. According
to Nyambara (2005), many Africans who were forcefully removed from the
Rhodesdale Estate resented the forceful relocation since they were prosperous
farmers with Master Farmer certificates and had adopted 'modern' ways
of agriculture and owned large herds of stock given the favourable climatic
conditions that obtained at Rhodesdale. Such people found themselves being
forcibly relocated to the dry and tsetse fly-ridden Gokwe area where they
struggled to re-establish their farming enterprises. Moreover, forced removals
dislocated families from their ancestors whose graves were left behind, livestock was lost and movable property also damaged during the process.

The Damvuri conservancy was one of the farms that was created after
Africans were forcefully removed from Rhodesdale in the 1940s. The conservancy was owned by Owain Lewis, a professional hunter who inherited
the land from his late parents. In terms of size, the conservancy comprised
two properties: Damvuri Ranch and the Rock Bar Ranch to the south of the
Muzvezve River which was acquired by Owain's family and incorporated into
Damvuri (see Figure 2). Before its occupation by war veteran-led peasants, the
conservancy was operated as a safari hunting business which specialized in
the lucrative but politically controversial trophy hunting industry. It attracted
wealthy American tourists who frequented the conservancy during the trophy
hunting seasons. By the time it was occupied in 2000, the Safari hunting
industry had already suffered as a result of a dramatic decline in the number
of safari hunting tourists due to political instability in the country. The
onset of land invasions and the global negative publicity they generated further damaged the already declining industry, thus making the safari hunting
business unsustainable and politically dangerous due to outbreaks of violence
in some occupied farms. Owain left Damvuri in 2000 after its occupation by

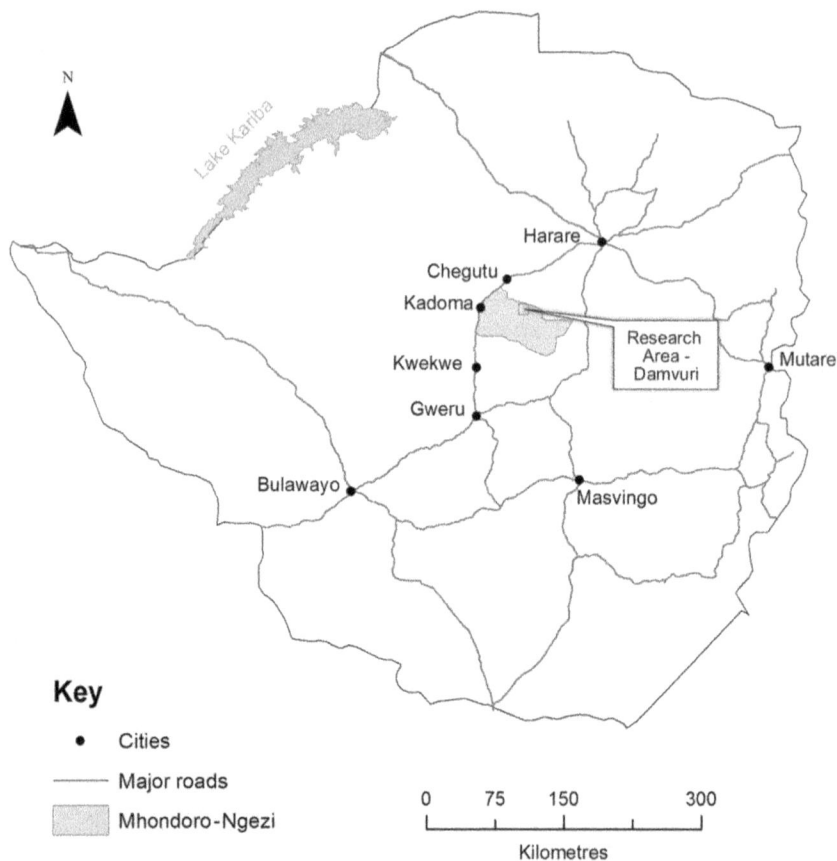

Figure 1 Location of the Study Area.

war veterans and it is rumoured that he bought a smaller piece of land in Darwendale near Harare where he is involved in some other business.

By the time of its occupation by war veterans in 2000, Damvuri conservancy had remained as an isolated white-owned safari hunting enclave in an area that had been largely 'acquired' and redistributed to peasant farmers. Most of the former white-owned farms and ranches in the broader area were acquired by the Government of Zimbabwe (GoZ) on a 'willing-seller willing-buyer' basis and turned into resettlement areas starting from the 1980s until the late 1990s. These developments left the Damvuri conservancy and a few white-owned properties in the area vulnerable to increased incidents of poaching of both fauna and flora and hence conflicts between peasant farmers from the nearby Mhondoro Ngezi CA and the Damvuri owner as noted by a former Damvuri worker:

Figure 2 The Former Damvuri Conservancy and Surrounding Farms.

By the time war veterans came to occupy Damvuri in 2000, Owain had already decided his safari operations were no longer sustainable because of poachers who came from nearby resettlement areas such as Tyron to the South, Bandahwe to the south east, Mopani plots to the west and Wale Ranch to the north; all these farms had been subdivided into plots under the Government of Zimbabwe's old resettlement schemes. (interview with Wisdom Mutanga at Damvuri on 07/08/2010)

Given the histories of forced removals and perceived white farmer injustices in the Mhondoro Ngezi area, land restitution discourses played a central role in the way people joined the occupation of white-owned farms. During interviews, the informants claimed that the reason they occupied white-owned land such as the Damvuri conservancy was that historically such lands belonged to their ancestors and that they had been forcibly evicted from the area. Moreover, histories of unjust treatment by white land owners played a role in the way some people joined the land occupations. For example, people from the Mhondoro Ngezi CA claimed that during the colonial era white land owners unfairly confiscated their livestock which had strayed into their private land. They further cited acts of injustices carried out by the white farmers such as brutal beatings of local people for petty crimes such as trespassing and natural resource poaching (snaring of wild animals, hunting with dogs and gathering of firewood) as reasons for their actions towards white farmers. Other informants cited historical grievances such as being barred from hunting while white land owners freely shot wild animals now fenced within private conservancies, excluding indigenous people from accessing such livelihoods.

In general, narratives of white farmer brutality were circulating in the local area way before farms were 'invaded' in 2000. Embedded within these narratives was a repertoire of metaphors which reflected historical tensions between Africans confined to ecologically degraded 'reserves' and their white neighbours who generally possessed better-quality land. Histories of white farmer brutality in Mhondoro Ngezi are reflected by nick names given to some white farmers. For example, the owner of Mopani Ranch which is located to the north of the Damvuri conservancy was renamed *mukanda bhutsu* (one who kicks), since the white owner had a reputation of kicking his workers or trespassers; the owner of Solitude Farm which is located to the east was called 'mhiripiri (Mr Hot Chillies), as the owner had a reputation for being temperamental, while the owner of Wale Ranch which is located to the west was called Rafu (Mr Rough) because of his reputation for being 'rough' with Africans who trespassed on his farm. Interviews provided below highlight how colonial-era injustices influenced the way people joined land occupations. Mr Phiri, a war veteran, was one of the first people who came to occupy the Damvuri conservancy in 2000. He came from the nearby old resettlement area of Tyron where he had owned a plot from the 1980s but decided that he needed more land as the area was now congested:

> During the Rhodesian times, white farmers had their own laws which
> they exercised with extreme brutality. The white farmer was a policeman,
> a magistrate, the judge and the prison guard. When these white farmers
> came to this area they were given executive powers by the Rhodesian

government to use force in order to make people work; it was generally believed that black people were lazy and that one needed to use force to make them work. The farmer paid very little in wages. During the liberation war the white farmer was a member of the Selous Scouts, that's why he always kept a gun. We came here to recover our ancestral lands lost to the whites. White farmers owned thousands of hectares of land while we were suffering in overcrowded reserves. There is nothing wrong with us taking back our land. (interview with Mr Phiri at Damvuri on 26/11/2010)

Mr Tichaona came to join the occupation of the Damvuri conservancy in 2001 from the nearby Mhondoro Ngezi CA; he had this to say about the former owner of the Damvuri conservancy:

The white farmer was cruel; he did not want to see a black person walking in the farm. If a man was seen walking along the road which goes through the farm, he was told to go back or he was going to be shot; many people were afraid of being shot by the farmer, he never wanted to see a black person with meat, he used to shoot dogs belonging to black people since he suspected them of being used for poaching. We came here in order to recover our land. We were suffering in Communal Areas, with no water and pasture for our livestock while farmers in this area were sitting on many acres of fertile land. We came here to take back our land from whites who abused us for many years. (interview with Mr Tichaona at Damvuri on 15/11/2010).

Mr Chipango, who came to Damvuri from Gokwe in 2003, claimed to have been evicted from the area by the Rhodesian government in the 1950s:

We were forcibly removed from our land by whites. They stole our livestock and other property during forced removals. Moreover, we were dumped in Gokwe, a hostile dry place with no water while whites gave themselves fertile land. This was no joke, people lost property such as livestock and other belongings. They came in the night, with very little warning and you were just told you are being moved to Gokwe. Old people were slapped by white boys. Boers are rubbish. We came here to recover our land. (interview with Chipango at Damvuri on 25/09/2010).

These commentaries highlight how colonial injustices influenced the way people joined land occupations in Mhondoro Ngezi. However, land occupations and resettlement in Mhondoro Ngezi oddly seemed to follow the old resettlement pattern in terms of the process being state-led and land claimants being registered with the DA before joining the land occupations. Unlike in many areas of Zimbabwe where war veterans had a free reign to occupy farms and redistribute land during the *jambanja* era, in Mhondoro Ngezi the process was state-led and followed a somewhat technocratic pattern from the beginning. Thus, the scenes of violence and chaos in occupied farms associated with the watershed moments of 2000 popularized by some scholars (Hammar 2003; Worby 2003) do not apply to the Mhondoro Ngezi situation. After occupying the Damvuri conservancy in 2000, war veterans were forced to work with state actors rather than bypass them. Their occupation remained a 'protest' until state structures came to legitimize it. Local state structures such as the DA and AREX Services, Kadoma Rural District Council and Ministry of Lands, which had long been involved in leading resettlement programmes in the early 1980s, were actively involved in the early stages of the occupation. The following section explores the dynamics of land occupations and the way authority over land was claimed and legitimized by the state.

Land Occupations and Their Dynamics in Mhondoro Ngezi

We came here through the struggle. (War Veterans leader interviewed on 13/06/2010)

Zimbabwe's war veterans were central in spearheading the land occupations after the 2000 benchmark. The role of war veterans and other non-state actors in these widespread land occupations has been extensively analysed in literature (Alexander 2003; Chaumba et al. 2003; Hammar 2003; Sadomba 2008). Any attempt to analyse and generalize the role of war veterans and ZANU PF structures during the land occupations is likely to face major challenges. This is simply because their role and influence were largely determined by local circumstances and contingency as there was no standard formula, which was followed in undertaking such occupations. In some places, war veterans emerged as powerful power brokers wielding enormous political authority. In other places, the state remained stubbornly in charge at a time when some commentators claimed the state had collapsed (Worby 2003; Richardson 2004). This inevitably makes findings based on one study area insufficient in generalizing trends and tendencies of fast track land reform processes and their subsequent outcomes.

Moreover, relationships between the various actors and their political roles and identities shifted with time; class conflicts, ethnicity and factionalism among such actors further complicated the situation. Geographical factors and local politics to some extent influenced how an invasion was undertaken, including its outcome. Moreover, the outcome of a land occupation also depended on the level of institutionalization of the state locally. The situation at the Damvuri conservancy defied the 'national' trend at many levels: state structures actively guarded against the occupation deteriorating into chaos; land seekers sought to formalize their land claims in the early stages rather than joining the 'illegal' occupation; the former owner was allowed to take away his property; and farm workers were not politically victimized and were allocated land like everyone else. This localized experience complicates attempts to make any generalizations in terms of how invasions took place and their outcomes, and it also questions popularized claims of chaos, state collapse (Hammar et al. 2003, 2010) and undue agency attributed to war veterans and other rural actors in recent literature on land reform (Sadomba 2010).

One of the major criticisms of the FTLRP programme was that during land occupations, local state institutions were undermined by war veterans and ZANU PF youths. According to Alexander,

> Land occupations required an extreme attack on institutions of the state, in very sharp contrasts to the government's response to the occupations in the 1980s when it had sought to strengthen and insulate a modernising bureaucracy. In 2000 the judiciary was severely undermined as ruling after ruling was ignored. The police force was increasingly politicised, purged of critics and prevented from carrying their duties [...] civil servants came under tremendous pressure to support ZANU PF and came under violent attack where they did not. The ministries charged with agrarian policy were meanwhile marginalised from control of land policy in favour of an alliance led by ZANU PF and War Veterans. (2003: 104)

While such a broad analysis gives a generalized picture of the political environment that underpinned fast track land reform, it also raises serious conceptual challenges in terms of how one can better understand the often localized and nuanced experiences in terms of how individual farms located in often diverse locations were occupied and demarcated and the role of various actors in such processes as Chaumba et al. have argued:

> The broad-brush representation of the farm invasion and fast track resettlement process as chaotic, violent, un-modern and unplanned obfuscates two overlapping phases underpinned by the same logic. Rather than constituting a descent into anarchy, the state bureaucracy

has been able to enact a rapid return to a 'technocratic type' – if indeed this type ever went away. (2003: 3)

Based on data gathered in Masvingo Province, Chaumba et al. (2003: 4) have demonstrated that the land occupations and subsequent allocations were already an ordered process during the so-called *jambanja* era as 'the occupiers often went to great length to employ the formal and technical tools of land use planning' and that 'the occupiers conducted their own survey and allocated plots'. This study is useful in the way it challenges the depiction of land occupations as chaotic. The way land occupations unfolded in Mhondoro Ngezi indicates that 'state modernism' and technocracy did not just 'return' after the occupation but were present from the beginning as the local state institutions such as the DA, AREX and Kadoma Rural District Council were actively involved in the early stages of the occupation facilitating the registration and transportation of land seekers to the occupied Damvuri conservancy.

Local ZANU PF activists, war veterans and the army (to a lesser extent) largely facilitated the mobilization of people and helped with logistics in conjunction with state structures such as the Kadoma Rural District Council. People from rural areas such as Sanyati and Gokwe (who constitute the majority of land beneficiaries) were mobilized and made to 'formally' register with the DA in Kadoma before they could be considered for land allocation. Although war veterans were central in organizing 'protests' such as leading the occupation of the Damvuri conservancy, their authority and political clout remained peripheral to that of local state actors who maintained a hegemonic presence during the occupation.

However, despite the hegemonic role played by the state during the land occupations, war veteran informants interviewed were keen to adopt the *jambanja* discourse in the way they sought to conceptualize the occupation of Damvuri. *Jambanja* appealed to them mainly because of its utility in their attempts to claim authority over land and that it was also a useful tool in their counterhegemonic struggles against state actors.

During interviews and informal conversations, war veterans were at pains to emphasize their important role during the occupation by appealing to broader liberation discourses. They interpreted their role as more of leading a revolution rather than mere facilitators of a state-led technocratic process. This was reflected in their rhetoric whenever they were given a chance to talk in public especially at local ZANU PF political meetings. They also claimed to have forced the Damvuri owner using military-style tactics, although this contradicts opinions of other informants such as the former farm workers and ordinary people.

Mr Munemo, a war veteran and one of the leaders of the occupation of the Damvuri conservancy, had this to say:

We came here through the struggle; we took over the farm because the white farmer was a cruel racist. We came to this farm in 2000. The white farmer tried to resist but we told him that this was our soil. We went to war for it. He tried to go to court and he also tried to get help from other white farmers but it did not work. We went to the DA's office in order to get more people to come and join the occupation, the DA had a list of people who had registered to get land, the people came from various areas but mostly from Gokwe who had lost their land during forced removals. These people wanted to come back home. The farm workers changed sides and joined the occupation when they realized that the farmer was going to lose the land. (interview at Damvuri on 10/10/2010)

Other war veterans were also eager to frame the occupation in military terms; for example, during the interviews they claimed that they expected the farmer to 'surrender' or give up arms. The farmer was also referred as a military 'target'. These militaristic discourses were repeatedly rehearsed during interviews with Mr Mujeki, a war veteran:

Land reform was a war. We fought for the land and without war whites were not going to surrender the land. Every Rhodesian farmer was a soldier, many of the farmers kept guns and as a result we treated them as soldiers. For us occupying the land was as good as going to war. We encouraged discipline as we were taught during the war, we were serious and ready to go to war. (interview at Damvuri on 10/10/2011)

War veteran militarism was further reflected in the way the 'Base' at Damvuri was organized; the base commander was by default the leader of the Committee of Seven (although this committee is largely symbolic at Damvuri) which was the administrative organ of the land occupiers. Moreover, war veterans sought to impose a strict military regime where they became de facto military commanders. They also acted as the police (a role they were assigned by the DA before the demarcation of Damvuri), with the youth, women and other 'civilians' being forced to observe a strict military code of conduct including regular drilling and rehearsals of *Chimurenga* songs. An informant who joined the war veterans in the early days of the occupation had this to say:

When we came here in 2000, it was like a war, we used to sing liberation songs all night, war veterans were the big guys, we waited for them to give us land, and they were in charge of food rationing and settling disputes and criminal justice. However, everybody was not allowed to touch anything belonging to the farmer until the DA came. (interview with Mr Mutaka on 8/10/2010)

Discourses of *chimurenga* (liberation war) reflected in several interviews go against counter-narratives of what happened during the land occupations. As highlighted earlier, although war veterans were central in the occupation of Damvuri, their activities were severely restricted by the involvement of the DA and other state structures such as AREX and the Kadoma District Council which did not allow the situation to deteriorate into a *'jambanja* phase'. According to such counter-narratives, the DA is claimed to have imposed a moratorium on hunting and other illegal activities such as interference with the white landowner's property until he had taken his property off the occupied land. This counter-narrative was not popular with war veteran informants who instead favoured the *jambanja* discourse which they sought to popularize in the early stages of the land occupations. During interviews, war veterans depicted the land occupations as *kutora nyika* (taking the country) rather than reclaiming the land. Such claims of 'liberating the country' resonated strongly with land-hungry people, especially in the early stages of the land reform. Such rhetoric was also key in the way war veterans sought to legitimize their activities and claims of authority over occupied land, as Mr Shangari, a war veteran leader, put it:

We came here to take the country that had been taken by Boers; these whites had kept our land since 1980 when we got independence. As former freedom fighters we remained in rural enclaves suffering without land. When the chance to get back the country came, we did not waste time because we thought enough is enough. (interview at Damvuri on 15/10/2011)

War veterans also attempted to take advantage of the absence of chiefly authority in the occupied area as chiefs Benhura, Nyika and Ngezi, who claimed to have some jurisdiction over it, did not join the land occupation but remained in the Mhondoro Ngezi CA. However, the presence of state structures meant that even though 'chiefly' authority was absent, it did not mean war veterans had a free reign to exercise authority over the newly occupied area. Local government structures remained in control over the affairs of the newly occupied area in terms of who could access the land and on what basis as a Ministry of Lands officer put it:

This farm was redistributed according to the law. The DA came here soon after the war veterans camped here. We did not allow disorder.

People had to go and register at the DA's office before coming here. That's why you see this area does not have the chaos reported elsewhere. (interview with Mujakachi at Damvuri on 06/02/2011).

Damvuri did not experience the total collapse or absence of state structures as claimed by some scholars (Worby 2003). The state was present in the beginning and it continues to be present well after the occupation. The relatively orderly transfer of property from the former owner to ordinary people can be attributed to the involvement of state structures in the early stages of the occupation as observed by a former farm worker:

The war veterans came and camped by the farm shop, there were no incidents of violence or confrontation between the war veterans and the farmer. The process involved a smooth handover of the farm facilitated by the DA. The former owner transported his animals to Rio Tinto where he had bought a plot as well as Pamuzinda Safari Lodge. He was also able to take away most of his personal belongings except the water tank. (interview with Mutanga at Damvuri on 23/09/2010)

The presence of state structures (and hence absence of *jambanja*) meant that the war veterans were not able to significantly influence and reshape authority structures as their role remained largely symbolic. Their influence seemed to have remained peripheral in terms of their ability to redistribute land as Ministry of Lands officials and AREX officers took centre stage in the demarcation of occupied land into individual plots. Thus, war veterans became mere facilitators of the process rather than running the show and also lacked the prestige and authority enjoyed by their counterparts elsewhere. State presence in the early stages of the occupation meant few opportunities to loot property and to acquire assets such as the 'homestead' (former farm house) which became public property (it houses civil servants such as AREX officers) rather than being a de facto home of the base commander as reported elsewhere (Scoones et al. 2010).

Moreover, the war veterans did not get preferential treatment in terms of plot sizes or quality of plots. At Damvuri, getting a plot was based on the concept of *kunhonga chijeke* (picking a bottle top), a process which involved technocrats from AREX and Ministry of Lands who pegged plots and assigned them with numbers. Such plot numbers were then placed in a box and land seekers were then asked to randomly pick a bottle top with a plot number from a bucket. The process of 'picking a bottle top' was designed to discourage people from picking and choosing specific pieces of land or getting larger pieces of land. This ordered process was resented by war veterans who expected certain privileges in the land allocation process given their 'assumed' role in leading land occupations. Some informants claimed that two war veteran leaders, Cde Urombo and Cde Jongwe, who were part of the group that spearheaded the occupation, reportedly left Damvuri in protest against state control of the process. A key informant representing government at the time had this to say:

> Here people were given land according to the law. The government was responsible for land redistribution. War veterans and others helped with logistics and keeping law and order. (interview with Gotora at Damvuri on 12/11/2010)

The centrality of technocracy and bureaucratic protocol during land occupations in Mhondoro Ngezi is reflected by the life histories of individual farmers gathered during the fieldwork. These biographies highlight how the land occupations and land allocations followed a rather bureaucratic trajectory rather than the *jambanja* which was popular in the early stages of the land reform programme.

Mrs Eva Ndlovu who was allocated land at the Damvuri conservancy had this to say about how she came to Damvuri:

> I came from Sanyati through the DA's office. My parents moved to Sanyati in the 1950s. They were coming from Rhodesdale near Kwekwe where they had been forcibly removed by white settlers. I got this farm on 11 November 2000 and then began building, and we were transported from Kadoma in army vehicles. (interview at Damvuri on 22/11/2010)

Another informant, Mr Lozane who came from Sanyati, also highlighted the centrality of the DA's office in the way he came to the Damvuri conservancy:

> My family came from Sanyati. Our parents say they were forcefully relocated from Rhodesdale near Kwekwe. We applied to the DA to get land here and we were allocated. We came on our own. Sanyati was too small for our growing family. There is plenty of land here and grazing pastures, we feel lucky that we are here although there are still problems related to being a new place. (interview at Damvuri on 22/11/2010)

Mrs Beatrice Ngwerengwe is an urbanite who left Kadoma town to join the occupation at the Damvuri conservancy. Her story further highlights the importance of the DA's office in the way people were allocated land at the Damvuri conservancy.

We came from Kadoma in 2000 through the DA's office. We went to register our interest for land and when an opportunity arose we were offered land here at Damvuri. My family is originally from Zimuto in Masvingo. Kadoma was expensive (rent, food, etc), we could not make ends meet. We came here to do farming to get food and income without anybody forcing or pushing you like we did in Kadoma. The agricultural situation is good here; we can manage to get food and then sell extra to get some income. (interview at Damvuri on 22/11/2010)

These testimonies highlight the centrality of the DA's office in the way people were allocated land at the Damvuri conservancy. The presence of local state institutions in the early stages of land occupations meant that land seekers sought to formalize their claims over land in the beginning rather than wait for the so-called planning phase (Chaumba et al. 2003). Another aspect of state hegemony reflected at Damvuri is the extent to which the state was able to maintain order after the farm occupation. For example, the former Damvuri owner was reportedly given a three-month notice by the DA to move his private property including 'his' wild animals, a privilege that was not enjoyed by other white farmers elsewhere. Contrary to war veterans' claims of having 'forced' the farmer off the land, he is reported to have been present (at the DA's invitation) during the official demarcation of Damvuri and is said to have lobbied the DA to give his former farm workers first preference in land allocations. Moreover, the former farm workers claim that their former employer continues to visit them 10 years after he left Damvuri, although they have discouraged him from visiting due to the security risk he poses. This illustrates the often-nuanced dynamics associated with the land occupations across Zimbabwe's countryside. It also demonstrates that the land occupations did not follow any particular phases and that in some places land occupations were a planned affair from the beginning. Moreover, claims of state collapse and chaos across the Zimbabwean countryside popularised in literature are too general and need to be qualified. Events at Damvuri demonstrate that state structures were not only present but also had an upper hand during the land occupation. Thus, it seems the cult of the war veteran as an outlaw imposing arbitrary authority in occupied areas popularized in the media and academic literature does not sufficiently capture the whole picture and is not pervasive. For example, a visitor to the former Damvuri conservancy is welcomed by a sign post reflecting modernist ideas about development rather than mob rule: *Welcome to Damvuri ...: Fast tracking education for development.*

At local ZANU PF political meetings which I attended during the field-work, 'modernist' ideas of 'development' and 'progress' were reflected in slogans which seem to castigate those who are against order and progress:

Forward with togetherness! Forward

Forward with Development! Forward

Down with those against development! Down.
          (recorded at a ZANU PF meeting at Damvuri on 23/07/2010)

This further highlights that land occupations and resettlement in Mhondoro Ngezi followed a logic different from that of *jambanja* which was popular at the time. It also highlights that newly resettled areas are ordered spaces largely influenced by discourses of development and progress which are supported by the state. Although war veterans attempted to depict farm occupations as *kutora nyika* (taking the country) as a way of leveraging authority over the newly occupied land, such attempts were hardly successful in overriding or under-mining the authority of local state institutions such as the DA and AREX. This does not mean to say their political influence can be totally dismissed, since they remain key figures in the way the state seeks to exercise authority over the area. To a large extent, they have been largely co-opted to operate side by side with official authority structures such as ward development committees (WADCOs), village development committees (VIDCOs), village heads and councillors. This dynamic interaction between the state and non-state actors in terms of how authority is exercised requires a better and more nuanced understanding of how the state functions and interacts with non-state actors as James Ferguson argues:

> We must not think of the new organisations [...] not as challengers pressing up against the state from below, but as horizontal contempor-aries of the organs of the state, sometimes rivals, sometimes servants, sometimes watchdogs, sometimes parasites but in every case operating on the same level and in the same [...] space. (2006: 103)

Within Damvuri, the boundaries between the state and non-state authorities are sometimes blurred, the former with an upper hand in the way the affairs of the area are run and the later regularly functioning as a mobilizing force during the elections in a largely patron–client set-up. The Damvuri experi-ence requires that we move away from 'totalizing' claims of state 'presence' and 'absence' or 'displacement' and 'chaos' during land occupations, but to critically engage with empirical evidence on the ground and to appreciate the diversity of experiences, as Ferguson (2006: 112) has argued: 'What is called for in other words is an approach to the state that would treat its verticality and encompassment not as a taken-for-granted fact but a precarious achievement.'

It also requires that we re-engage with debates about the nature of the postcolonial state in sub-Saharan Africa, in particular its partial institutional-ization and how that has an impact on operations of state institutions as noted by Chabal and Daloz:

> The origins of African polities tend to confuse appearance with reality. The fact that all post-colonial states have been formally constituted on the modern Western state is not in itself evidence of the degree of their institutionalisation. Above and beyond the public display of the attributes of the modern state [...] the reality of the exercise of power on the continent points to a necessary caution when it comes to assessing the degree to which such formal bodies do amount to a modern (Weberian) state. (1999: 8)

There is an increasing need to problematize the often-unwarranted agency attributed to war veterans in literature on fast track land reform (Sadomba 2010) and to re-engage with theories that question the 'total' institutionaliza-tion of the state in Africa (Chabal and Daloz 1999; Ferguson 2006). These can provide practical answers in the way in which one can explain the 'spatial' character of the state which was reflected in the way in which the state seemed to be 'present' in some places regulating the actions of the local actors while at some places its 'absence' resulted in local actors temporarily taking charge of key state functions such as land redistribution.

The Damvuri case study has highlighted the spatialized nature of the state in terms of how it interacted with local actors in various locations across the country. It also demonstrates that although local actors such as war veterans were central in spearheading land occupations, the state remained the 'legit-imate' arbiter of land rights playing a hegemonic role in such processes. Non-state actors had to work with the state rather than bypass it. War veterans' claims of having forced the farmer off Damvuri in a *jambanja*-style operation are largely exaggerated. Evidence on the ground indicates that although they were instrumental in organizing 'protests' such as the occupation of Damvuri, the occupation did not result in a total breakdown of law which would have allowed widespread looting of property and the dominance of new forms of authority as claimed elsewhere (Hammar et al. 2003). Although new forms of authority such as war veterans and the Committee of Seven are now a key part of local authorities, even though their authority and influence as independent entities is largely symbolic, they function as an informal extension of local state structures.

Farm Workers and Land Occupations in Mhondoro Ngezi

One of the major criticisms of the fast track land reform programme was its impact on the livelihoods of farm workers, particularly how land occupations resulted in them not only losing employment but also being evicted after a farm had been occupied (Alexander 2003; Rutherford 2003). It has also been claimed that farm workers were politically victimized (because of their presumed association with the farmer) and thus became internally displaced people. While my aim is not to dismiss such claims, I intend to problematize them at two levels: first, such claims need to be qualified since they do not sufficiently capture the dynamic interaction among various actors during land occupations across the Zimbabwean countryside. Second, such claims take away agency from farm workers by depicting them as passive victims of a changing agrarian situation. Below I will analyse the experiences of farm workers in Mhondoro Ngezi and try to locate them in a broader context of fast track land reform.

Most of the former workers at the Damvuri conservancy were of foreign origin (mainly Zambian and Malawian) and had worked at the conservancy for a relatively long time (on average about 10 years). Some of them had worked for Owain Lewis's father in the 1970s, and later for Owain up until 2000 when Damvuri was occupied by war veterans. The conservancy had very little crop and livestock production, thus the work force was relatively small (an estimated 20–40 workers). Most of the workers were game rangers and general labourers; a few had specialist skills such as skinning and taxidermy which were essential in the safari hunting trade. Most of the workers with specialist skills opted to leave the conservancy with their employer rather than remain to become peasant farmers.

The relatively peaceful occupation of Damvuri seemed to have been a favourable outcome for the former workers. Most of them (93 per cent according to the Damvuri survey) benefited from land reform except for a few (7 per cent) who decided to go with their employer. The experience of these former workers contrasts significantly with that of farm workers elsewhere where widespread victimization of farm workers was recorded during farm occupations (Rutherford 2001, 2003). There are various reasons for this, the most significant one being the involvement of key state actors such as the DA, Ministry of Lands officials and the police in the early stages of the occupation. Another reason mentioned by former farm workers during the fieldwork was that their previous employer negotiated with the DA for them to be given land after his departure and was even present to witness them *vachinhonga chijeke* (picking bottle tops with plot numbers).

The experience of farm workers in Mhondoro Ngezi demonstrates the often nuanced and localized experiences in individual farms and across the Zimbabwean rural landscape. At Damvuri, for example, in the aftermath of land reform, such former workers are among those who are economic-ally doing well, having acquired property such as tractors, livestock and built better-looking houses than those who came from CAs. These former farm workers seem to have capitalized on their knowledge of the place and the technical skills they acquired during their time as farm workers. The biog-raphies of the former farm workers below highlight their experience, particu-larly the way in which land occupations unfolded allowed them access to land. They also highlight how in some places white land owners negotiated with local state structures to be allowed to leave the land peacefully and at times even secured land for their former employees before they left. Mr Mabheka, who came from the Mhondoro Ngezi CA and worked for the Damvuri con-servancy for 20 years as a cook, had this to say about life at the conservancy before land occupations:

> Owain, the Damvuri owner, had a good relationship with us. He used to allow us to grow our own crops on one-acre plots and encouraged us by giving us seeds and fertilisers. At times, he would help us with tilling. When he left, he gave us pension money and livestock. I was given one cow and some money. He also made sure we benefited from land reform after he left. (interview at Damvuri on 23/06/2010)

Although some informants who came from nearby Mhondoro Ngezi CA and old resettlement schemes claimed that Owain was a bad neigh-bour who deserved to be evicted, such perspectives are contradicted by his former workers who claim that he kept a relatively good relationship with his neighbours despite many of them poaching animals at the conservancy. They also claim that he contributed to political events in the Mhondoro Ngezi CA by donating meat and other commodities during national events such as Heroes and Independence Day celebrations as noted by Mr Mutanga who was a manager at Damvuri before land occupations:

> Owain maintained good relations with his neighbours from nearby communal areas such as Mhondoro Ngezi. People would come to ask for meat donations during national events such as Independence and Heroes days. Owain never instructed us to beat or kill locals, he always

instructed us to arrest the poachers or shoot their dogs. (interview with Mutanga at Damvuri on 23/06/2010)

Former workers also highly appreciated the fact that when Owain decided to leave Damvuri, he gave them some small pension in the form of livestock and farm implements to help them start their new life as peasant farmers. This helped them with start-up capital as one former worker put it:

> When Owain was about to leave he went to the DA and pleaded with him in order to ensure that we were also given land. When land was being allocated, he was actually present witnessing the process. Moreover, before the farm was taken, he used to lend us his tractor for us to plough our one acre stands. He gave us inputs such as fertilisers and seeds. He also gave us livestock and other implements to help start our farming operations. (interview with Mutanga at Damvuri on 23/06/2010)

There are various reasons why these former workers seemed sympathetic towards their former employer, a few of which I will highlight below. Most of these former workers were of foreign origin and they faced the prospect of destitution if they were not given land after their employer had left. Hence, they appreciated the noble gesture of their employer for looking after them during a period of socio-economic uncertainty. Although such former workers were largely sympathetic towards their former employer, this did not however mean they were against his departure. During interviews, they were quick to say that it was better that their former employer left. They also appreciated having somewhere that they call their own rather than working since their former employer did not allow them to own land as reported thus:

> Life has improved for me and my family; it is very different being entirely dependent on someone for survival. When Owain was here we were not allowed to keep livestock such as goats and cows, but now we have the freedom. (interview with Mutanga at Damvuri on 23/08/2010)

The way in which these former farm workers narrate their experiences brings new perspectives which are missing in current literature on land reform and broadens our understanding of the impact of fast track land reform on the former farm workers. Rather than looking at such former workers as victims of land reform and hence taking away their agency during the farm occupations, they could be viewed as active participants in an unfolding agrarian situation. Moreover, we should also appreciate that their experiences varied from one place to the other. Although many of these former workers were sympathetic to their employer, it seemed such sympathies did not amount to them wishing the farm was not taken for resettlement. They supported fast track land reform mainly because it opened up opportunities to own land. Moreover, since most of these workers were of foreign ancestry, many of them had no *kumusha* (rural homes) where they could go when unemployed, retired, old or infirm as noted by an informant during interviews:

> We have a better life, working for another person is problematic, you are always afraid of what happens if you lose your job. We now have our own homes and somewhere to live. (interview with Chioso at Damvuri 22/04/2011)

These interviews demonstrate that not all farm workers were victims of a changing agrarian situation, but were active participants who utilized the opportunities available to them during the land occupations. Such former workers saw the onset of fast track land reform as an opportunity to officialize their 'local' identity having established stronger roots with the local area; this is explored in in detail in Chapter 3. Former farm workers had been in an identity limbo and had been labelled *vanhu vasina musha* (people without homes) which made it difficult for them to belong to the local area. Thus, such farm workers appreciated the freedom to own a home and to belong somewhere rather than live in the farm compound.

Conclusion

The way the land occupations unfolded in Mhondoro Ngezi demonstrates that land occupations unfolded in diverse ways across Zimbabwe's countryside. Although war veterans led the land occupations at the Damvuri conservancy in 2000, the occupation did not result in widespread violence or breakdown of law and order as witnessed in other parts of Zimbabwe. Farm workers were not blatantly victimized or evicted by war veterans as claimed elsewhere, but benefited from land reform and became key members of the new community. The former white land owner did not suffer the level of political victimization suffered by other farmers elsewhere, and was even allowed some time to take away most of his private property before the farm was officially demarcated. Moreover, the state was present in the process and acted as a controlling agent imposing law and order rather than allowing the total deterioration of the occupation into social disorder and political chaos. Thus, the occupation was more of a state-led technocratic process where the DA, AREX and Ministry of Lands officials led the demarcation of the occupied land into individual plots.

One of the major dynamics of the fast track land reform widely popularized in literature is how the state was 'unravelled' as war veterans and other non-state actors such as ZANU PF structures bypassed the state institutions as they assumed authority to redistribute land. This process, it is claimed, involved, inter alia, the breakdown of law and order, wanton destruction of property, gross human rights abuses and displacement and victimization of former farm workers. However, such claims cannot be generalized and do not sufficiently provide a complete picture. The Mhondoro Ngezi experience demonstrates that the state was not always absent in the process of land reform, as it retained a high level of hegemony over how land claims were made, processed and legitimized. War veterans did not have a free reign to take the law into their own hands and impose a new form of 'order' free from state control. Moreover, the occupation and subsequent demarcation of land into individual plots was a 'modern' technocratically driven process overseen by state structures. Former farm workers were not victims of land reform, but they were allowed to register with the DA and were allocated land. This chapter demonstrates that the dynamics of land occupations are quite nuanced and that the state is still seen as the 'legitimate' arbiter of land rights. War veterans and other non-state actors have been largely co-opted to work with the state rather than undermine it.

Chapter 3

LAND BENEFICIARIES AND THEIR ORIGINS

People who were resettled at the former Damvuri conservancy in Mhondoro Ngezi are not by any means a homogeneous group. They can be grouped into three broad categories based on where they came from. First, there are those who came from the low-lying areas of Sanyati and Gokwe who constitute the majority of the land beneficiaries at Damvuri. Second, there are former residents of the nearby Mhondoro Communal Area (CA) and the old resettlement areas within the vicinity. The third and last group consists of people from the gold and platinum mines in the broader Mhondoro Ngezi area, the urban areas of Kadoma, Kwekwe and Chegutu, former farm workers from the Damvuri conservancy and other former large-scale commercial farms (LSCF) in the area. It is important to highlight here that land reform was a process rather than a one-off event; some people belong to the same category, but having acquired land at different moments of the land reform process. Some were the so-called pioneers who joined the initial war veteran-led occupation in 2000, while others came later during the planning phase after 2004. Moreover, these broad categories constitute people of different age groups, gender, social and economic backgrounds. It is important to highlight here that women were allocated land in their own right. This was especially the case for widows and other unmarried women who joined land occupations. Those who were married but whose husbands were either working in cities or in the diaspora were also allocated land and their names appear on the land 'Offer Letter'.

The way people joined the land occupations at the Damvuri conservancy varied depending on their place of origin. Those who came from areas further away from the Mhondoro Ngezi District such as Sanyati and Gokwe mostly followed a rather formal process by registering their interest in land either through local war veterans or the ZANU PF local branch in their place of origin. Such people then organized themselves into groups and travelled to the town of Kadoma where they camped at the district administrator's (DA's) office for 'processing' before they were transported to the Damvuri conservancy. Such a process took days or weeks before people were finally resettled. Those who were already on the waiting list were contacted by the DA's office and allocated land.

Those who came from areas near the Damvuri conservancy, such as residents of the Mhondoro Ngezi CA, old resettlement areas in Mhondoro Ngezi District, former farm workers, urbanites and miners, simply joined the war veterans who had occupied the conservancy and thereafter formally registered their interest for land. Due to the bureaucratic nature of land occupations in Mhondoro Ngezi, those who joined the occupation directly were also registered with the DA's office in Kadoma before they were allocated land. Below I provide an analysis of how people in these broad categories came to join land occupations at the Damvuri conservancy and how people in various categories deployed various tactics to enhance their chances of accessing land. Land seekers often had to manoeuvre around a raft of political, bureaucratic, class and gender-based bottlenecks, in order to gain access to land.

Former Mhondoro Ngezi CA Residents

The Mhondoro Ngezi CA borders the former white-owned farms (LSCF) within which the Damvuri conservancy is located. CA people resettled at the conservancy came from the territories of chiefs Nyika, Benhura and Ngezi, within the Mhondoro Ngezi CA. The three chiefs did not directly participate in land occupations. Of the three of them, only Chief Nyika acquired an A2 plot (commercial farm) at the former Rock Bar Ranch, located on the southern part of the Damvuri conservancy. However, the three chiefs have made territorial claims over the former LSCF areas opened up by the fast track land reform process. There was no single motivating factor which influenced people in this group to join the land occupations. Informants in this category cited overcrowding, poor soils and the need for better pasture for livestock as reasons for joining the land occupations. However, some cited the recovery of ancestral lands lost during the colonial era-forced removals as a major factor. Due to the close proximity of the Mhondoro Ngezi CA to the former white-owned farms, such people historically believed that these were their ancestral lands alienated for European use during the colonial era, although such claims are contested. The Mhondoro Ngezi CA was a labour reserve situated in an area surrounded by white-owned farms endowed with the bulk of the best land surrounding the CA alienated for European use during the colonial era. Africans were squeezed into an area of predominantly poor coarse-grained sands with limited subsoil drainage. The soil structure in the area leads to a seasonal perched water table characterized by high levels of acidity and low base saturation, which impedes soil fertility and drainage (Andersen et al. 1993).

This poor ecological soil structure contrasts significantly with the former white farms nearby, where better soils and ecological conditions suited for both crop production and livestock production predominate. This contrast in the agroecological potential of the two areas and increasing overpopulation and ecological degradation in CAs was a major source of grievances among the former residents of the Mhondoro Ngezi CA. Such people resented the fact that while they were overcrowded in an ecologically degraded CA, the neighbouring white farms had large tracts of land which were visibly underutilized. Historically, Africans from the Mhondoro Ngezi CA deployed what Scott called 'weapons of the weak' (1986) such as illegally grazing their livestock in white-owned farms, poaching of game and other acts of sabotage such as cutting the game perimeter fence and snaring of wild animals as forms of resistance and diversification of livelihoods given the socio-economic and ecological conditions obtaining in CAs.

These 'illegal' activities generally strained the relationship between Africans in the Mhondoro Ngezi CA and their white neighbours in the nearby commercial farms. The ecological crises facing people in the CA and grievances against white landowners were key to the way people in this group joined the land occupations in 2000. According to interviews with informants, the killing of a CA resident by a white farmer on suspicion of poaching wildlife on his land is believed to have triggered the land occupations in the area in 2000.

The biographies[1] provided below highlight why and how people joined the farm occupations and where they came from. Some of the names of informants have been slightly changed to protect their identity.

Mr J. Machikiche came from Mamina in Chief Benhura's territory in the Mhondoro Ngezi CA. He and his wife came to the Damvuri conservancy in 2002 and were allocated a plot in Village 7:

> We came from Mhondoro Mamina in 2002; we did not have a piece of land to grow our own crops. During the liberation struggle we relocated to Lusaka in Zambia. We came back to Zimbabwe in 1980 and we had no land. We stayed at someone else's place. In Mhondoro Ngezi the small plot we owned barely produced 5 bags of maize, but now we produce many tonnes of maize. When we heard about availability of land at Damvuri, we went to register our names at the local ZANU PF

---

[1] The names of informants have been slightly altered to protect their identity.

office in Mamina. After registering we were told to go to Damvuri where we were allocated a plot. (interviewed at Damvuri on 21/06/2010)

Mrs Changi came from Chief Nyika's territory in Mhondoro Ngezi. She and her husband joined the occupation in 2000 in the early stages of the FTLRP and were allocated a plot in Village 8:

> We came from Bhururu in Mhondoro Ngezi in 2000. We were part of the very few people who joined land occupations at the beginning. When we came here, we did not completely give up our home in the Mhondoro CA. We wanted to be sure that this place was going to be secure enough before we completely gave up our home. In any case we still have relatives back there. The soils in Mhondoro were bad and unproductive. We also had three sons who needed land to start their own families. Our land back home was too small for a growing family. We were attracted by the good soils and rainfall patterns in the area. We also liked the plentiful pasture available here where our livestock can graze freely unlike in Mhondoro communal area where there is hardly any pasture for livestock. (interviewed at Damvuri on 18/06/2010)

Mrs Mangwiro came from Muchemwa in Chief Benhura's territory in the Mhondoro CA. She and her husband joined the occupation in 2002 and were allocated land in Village 7:

> We came to from Muchemwa in Chief Benhura's territory in Mhondoro Ngezi; we came here after people told us that there was land. The soils back there were tired. The place is overcrowded. This land belonged to our ancestors; white farmers were sitting on good quality land while we were stuck with poor soils. We came to recover our land. Before we came here, we registered with the DA in Kadoma and were offered a plot. This place has plentiful grazing pastures and more opportunities to do other things. Coming here was not very difficult since it's close to our place of origin. We used scotch carts to carry our belongings. We still have part of our family back in the communal areas although we gave up our plot. (interviewed at Damvuri on 17/06/2010)

These biographies highlight people's backgrounds and their motivations for seeking land. They also demonstrate that the need for better-quality land and pasture was some of the reasons for joining the land occupations. Due to the close proximity of the Mhondoro Ngezi CA to the Damvuri conservancy, it was generally easy for people to relocate. However, the relocation was staggered; men generally moved to Damvuri first and women and children remained behind but followed later when the basic facilities were in place. There were various reasons why people in this category kept their CA homes. First, it was a way of hedging for land in new areas and also maintaining their traditional homes as a security precaution. Second, some families sought to address the pressure for land in the CA by securing plots for their sons in the newly resettled area. Thus, some people in this category did not relocate to the new area; instead, such plots are being utilized by relatives some of whom were squatting on land.

Others, particularly the elderly people, were reluctant to completely abandon their homes since starting a new home was a laborious process requiring a big investment in manual labour. This process entailed clearing the virgin land and building new infrastructure such as houses, cattle pens and granaries. Moreover, such people had heavily invested in their CA homes; they had built 'modern'-looking bungalows and sanitary facilities such as toilets which they were reluctant to leave behind. Elderly people tended to have a strong sense of belonging to their old community where graves of ancestors were located and hence such graves could not be simply left behind. Moreover, maintaining land rights in both places was also a way of 'beating the system' as newly occupied areas such as the Damvuri conservancy were deemed 'contested' areas by international donors and food relief organizations and were thus excluded from their projects. Maintaining a CA home meant that one could access donor assistance directly or indirectly through family members who remained looking after the old homesteads. Thus, such donor services indirectly found their way to newly resettled areas through family networks. Availability of some social services and/or infrastructure in the CAs was another reason for people's reluctance to relocate to newly resettled areas and to maintain the CA homestead.

In general, people in this category did not have to sacrifice large amounts of resources in terms of logistics as it was easy for them to simply walk or use ox-drawn carts to transport their belongings to the newly resettled area. Moreover, such people were familiar with the ecological landscape in the occupied area and thus required less time to adjust as it was relatively close to their place of origin.

Gokwe and Sanyati 'Returnees'

Despite the relatively long distance between Gokwe and Mhondoro Ngezi District, people in this group constitute the majority of the people resettled at the Damvuri conservancy. But why and how did people in this category come to join the land occupations in Mhondoro Ngezi, an area which is located over two hundred kilometres away, rather than occupy farms closer to their places of origin? Various reasons were cited by informants in this category as to why they ended up at the Damvuri conservancy in Mhondoro Ngezi District. First, they claimed to have a historical connection with the area as they were part of a group of people who were forcibly evicted from the former Rhodesdale Estate by the colonial government in the 1960s. Second, some of them reported that they were attracted by better-quality land and the prospect of alternative livelihoods such as gold panning and working as wage labourers across gold and platinum mines located in the area.

But how did these people come to the Damvuri conservancy given the long distance between the two locations? In terms of logistics, coming to the Mhondoro Ngezi area was not necessarily easy for them. The long distance meant that they had to invest relatively large sums of money and time to move families after securing plots. This made it much more expensive to straddle between Gokwe and the newly occupied area in order to spread risks. As a result, whole families moved rather than splitting as in the case of those in the Mhondoro Ngezi category. Moreover, the remoteness of Gokwe meant that there was hardly any transport to the area since many public transport operators had been forced out of business due to severe fuel shortages which were experienced across Zimbabwe after 2000. Unlike their counterparts from the Mhondoro Ngezi CA, they were under much more pressure to gain access to land due to the fact that the overcrowding and land degradation experienced in Gokwe in the 1990s left many of them with limited options for alternative livelihood strategies. The cotton boom of the post-independence era which had attracted many immigrants from other parts of Zimbabwe had all but collapsed by the late 1990s. The situation was further worsened by recurrent droughts which led to frequent crop failure and low yields. Moreover, the skyrocketing inflation and the general slump in cotton prices undermined the peasant economy and forced people to look for alternative livelihoods else-where. The biographies[2] below highlight why people left Gokwe and Sanyati in search of land in Mhondoro Ngezi and the logistics involved in such a process.

Mr Madheu came to Damvuri from Chief Lozane's area of Sanyati in 2000. He was allocated a plot in Village 7:

> I came from Sanyati in 2000. My parents were born in Rhodesdale in this area, but were forcibly relocated to Gokwe by white settlers in the 1950s. We were cotton farmers in the Sanyati area. My father had ten

---

[2] The names of informants have been slightly altered to protect their identities.

children. In the beginning it was easier to grow crops, but it increasingly became difficult as the soil became infertile; droughts which led to successive poor harvest affected us. Moreover, our family grew in size and the demand for better quality land increased. I used to work in a supermarket at the Gokwe centre as a cashier but lost the job in 1998. I did not have land of my own, so my wife and I stayed with my parents. However, it was not easy to continue living with parents since I got married and had my own kids. The family homestead became congested; there was no land for all of us. I had one cow, which I sold in order for us to move here. I initially registered with Kadoma District Council in 1999 to be resettled and my name was put on a waiting list. I wanted to get land in this area because this is where my parents originally came from. My father used to talk about availability of land here, good soils and rainfall and other natural resources. In early 2000, I got a letter from Kadoma Rural Council informing me that a new farm had been opened up for resettlement. I joined a group of people and we camped at the Kadoma Rural District Council Offices before we organised transport to come here in March 2000. (interviewed at Damvuri on 24/10/2010)

Mr Mafamashiza came from Chief Nembudziya's territory in Gokwe in 2000. He was allocated a plot in Village 6:

We came from Nembudziya. My grandfather was born in Rhodesdale, but was forcibly moved to Sanyati in 1952. He then moved to Nembudziya to get better land for cotton growing. I grew up there although I left to work at Empress Mine in 1994. I am the first born in a family of 15 children since my father was a polygamist. I had a piece of land of my own and used to grow a variety of crops. I was doing well in Gokwe because I used to harvest a lot of cotton and made good money. This changed in the late 1990s when it became difficult to grow cotton since we had no money to buy chemicals and other farm implements. The market for cotton became so bad that it was not worth it. The major problem with Gokwe was that it is a dry area which suffers periodic droughts. Moreover, as a result of changing climate, the droughts increased in intensity which made life difficult for many farmers. In some years we had no water for consumption and for our livestock. I joined others who had registered their names with war veterans in order to be resettled. We used an army truck to come to Kadoma to join others who were waiting to come to Damvuri. We were brought here after some days of camping in Kadoma at the DA's office where our names were registered. (interviewed at Damvuri on 24/10/2010)

These biographies provide a picture of people's socio-economic situation before they moved from Gokwe and Sanyati. They also reflect changing livelihood trajectories associated with climate change and the 'boom and bust' cotton economy of Gokwe which forced people to seek better land elsewhere. There are three fundamental characteristics of people in this group which are worth mentioning. First, the people in this group took bigger risks in order to gain access to land in Mhondoro Ngezi given the long distances between the two locations. Second, the remote location of Gokwe meant that people had to invest relatively large amounts of resources in order to move their families and property at a time when transport was generally difficult to organize due to shortages of fuel. Third, the long distance between Gokwe and the newly occupied area made it difficult to straddle between the two locations in order to spread risks and to utilize family connections in terms of labour and other social support mechanisms.

Another important logistical dynamic highlighted by informants during interviews was the fact that people in this category had to undertake many tasks simultaneously such as clearing the land, building houses and cattle pens as families had to be moved all at once due to transport costs. Some of the tasks such as building houses and planting crops had to be undertaken concurrently given the fact that some people moved just before the rainy season. It was generally difficult for them to leave some of their family members behind as a risk aversion strategy given the long distance between the newly resettled area and their places of origin. This meant that they did not enjoy the support of their relatives and social networks like their counterparts from the Mhondoro Ngezi CA. An important social characteristic of this group is that a large number of them claim an autochthonous connection with the Mhondoro Ngezi area. During interviews and informal conversations, informants in this category tended to conceptualize fast track land reform as a form of land restitution since it had allowed them to recover ancestral lands lost during the colonial era.

Farm Workers, Urbanites and Mine Workers

There has been a general tendency in literature on Zimbabwe's land reform (Rutherford 2001; Hammar et al. 2010) to take away agency from farm workers by projecting them as passive victims of a changing agrarian structure who have become internally displaced people as a result of the land reform. Empirical evidence on the ground (Chambati and Magaramombe 2008; Chambati 2011; Mkodzongi 2013; AIAS Survey 2014) suggests that farm workers were active participants in the politics of land rather than merely victims, and that in some places, for example, at the Damvuri conservancy, former farm workers benefited from the land reform and have become key members of the newly resettled community. Land reform provided farm workers with an opportunity to gain access to land and other assets such as livestock and equipment, which their former employer could not take away. These assets gave the farm workers a form of start-up capital to begin their new life as peasant farmers.

There is a need to disaggregate farm workers in terms of citizenship and geographical location, since lumping them into one group masks variations in their socio-economic circumstances and hence their ability to deal with the changing agrarian structure. For example, disaggregating the farm worker category helps us to understand variations in the way they were affected by land occupations. During the land reform, some farm workers were better off than others and had the means to hedge against the risks associated with land reform. Some were highly skilled and were able to acquire land and are now part of agrarian elite, whereas some were more vulnerable than others, especially the female and migrant farmer workers (Moyo et al. 2009). Former farm workers of foreign origin were much more vulnerable since losing jobs meant that they were likely to become homeless as they did not have land rights in CAs. However, local farm workers had the option to simply go back to their CAs where they had homes and land (Scoones et al. 2010). These variations in farm workers' circumstances require a more nuanced analysis in order to better understand the impact of the changing agrarian situation to their livelihoods.

It is important to highlight that the fate of farm workers was largely determined by local political dynamics that underpinned the occupation of individual farms. There were variations in the way in which a farm was occupied (Scoones et al. 2010); in some places, farm workers fought pitched battles with war veterans in defence of their employer and hence their livelihoods. In other places, a farm occupation was initiated by farm workers with the help of war veterans, and in other places farm workers were evicted together with their former employer, especially if they refused to support war veterans or were suspected of being anti-ZANU PF.

The experience of farm workers in Mhondoro Ngezi was largely influenced by the relatively peaceful transfer of the occupied land to the government for redistribution and the intervention of their former employer who was able to lobby the DA to give them land after he left. Farm workers were thus not victims of the land reform process as witnessed elsewhere, but emerged better-off as they had no land of their own before and relied on wage employment for their livelihoods. Although the farm workers lost jobs as a result of land reform, those interviewed during fieldwork were happy to have been allocated land and the fact that they were no longer bonded at the farm as labourers with no land of their own. A few biographies provided below highlight the situation of farm workers at the Damvuri conservancy during the reform process.

Mr Mutanga came from Zambia in the 1970s and worked at the Damvuri conservancy as manager until its occupation by war veterans in 2000. He had this to say about his experience:

> I came from Zambia as an immigrant, I used to work for the elder Lewis before he died and then I worked for his son Owain who inherited the Damvuri farm which he converted into a conservancy in the 1980s. Working for a white farmer was always a challenge as the wages were always low. As a manager I enjoyed certain benefits such as access to small loans, a small plot to grow crops. I also had better accommodation compared to my subordinates. When land occupations occurred we were nervous that war veterans were going to evict us. However, the involvement of ZANU PF politicians and the DA in Kadoma protected us. We were allocated land like everyone else despite the fact that some of us are of foreign origin. I am happy with the land reform process, now I have land of my own and have somewhere to call home. (interviewed at Damvuri on 23/09/2010)

John Mabheka came from Mhondoro Ngezi in Chief Nyika's territory. He used to work as a game ranger at the Damvuri conservancy until the land occupations in 2000. He had this to say about the land reform process:

> I came from the local area in the nearby Mhondoro Ngezi CA. I worked as a game ranger here for five years. The white owner of this farm was a temperamental guy who was very unpredictable. Working for him was always a challenge. He was not always bad as he would give us meat during the hunting season. I also used to get tips from hunting tourists which provided a bit of extra income. However, working for a white landowner meant that we did not get good wages. The little money I got I sent it back to my wife in the communal areas where she paid school fees for our kids and bought food. I was happy when war veterans came here. I wanted land here as it is more fertile than the land in the Mhondoro Reserve. Without land reform I could still be working for peanuts. (interviewed at Damvuri on 23/09/2010)

These biographical summaries show how the land reform in Mhondoro Ngezi allowed former farm workers to access land. They also highlight that farm workers received subsistence wages which did not meet their needs, thus they welcomed the land reform process despite the job losses. According to these former workers, the impact of losing jobs was minimal given the fact that they benefited from gaining land as they now owned plots. Moreover, such former farm workers are now more mobile and able to pursue other alternative livelihoods when farming is not viable, as they are now free.

Data from the Mhondoro Ngezi case study demonstrate that fast track land reform provided vulnerable groups such as farm workers and wage labourers of foreign origin with an opportunity to own a piece of land. Such land provided them with a *musha* (home) where they could live an independent life as peasant farmers rather than relying on wage labour alone for their livelihoods. The experience of farm workers and other landless groups in Mhondoro Ngezi contrasts significantly with trends observed elsewhere where a more violent stand-off and takeover of farms resulted in farm worker displacement. The Mhondoro Ngezi experience highlights that farm workers were not only victims of the land reform process but also utilized whatever opportunities at their disposal to gain access to land during a changing agrarian situation.

Were the Beneficiaries ZANU PF Supporters?

One of the claims made by critics of Zimbabwe's fast track land reform was that it mainly benefited ZANU PF cronies (Hammar et al. 2003; Zamchiya 2011). While this claim cannot be simply dismissed, the situation on the ground was rather nuanced, thus making it difficult for anybody to make sweeping generalizations. There is a near global agreement among scholars that access to the more lucrative A2 (commercial farms) required political connections (Moyo et al. 2009; Scoones et al. 2010; Matondi 2012; Mkodzongi 2013); however, the situation was rather different with the A1 sector. Interviews with resettled farmers in Mhondoro Ngezi show that although land seekers often instrumentalized ZANU PF membership as a way of gaining access to land or protecting themselves from political violence during the land occupations, such people cannot simply be labelled 'ZANU PF cronies'. Such a categorization is problematic as the situation on the ground was rather complicated.

During my field work in Mhondoro Ngezi, the question, 'are you a member of ZANU PF or not', seemed to surprise my research informants. This was because to most of them, the concept of being ZANU PF was rather relative. People did not attach a lot meaning to their ZANU PF membership beyond its utility in allowing them access to land. As one of my informants remarked, 'It is common sense to be a member of ZANU PF for the simple reason that if you are perceived not to be a member, your chances of getting land are slim' (Mr Chikonzi interviewed on 20/11/2010). A result of the above was that ZANU PF membership was 'performed' out of necessity rather than genuine. This does not mean there were no so-called genuine supporters of

ZANU PF (if there is such a thing); what is argued here is that ZANU PF membership was relative. Among my informants were people who were not only outwardly ZANU PF but also secretly confessed to belong to the MDC political party or did not belong to any political party. Others did not belong to any political party but carried the ZANU PF party card and attended political party meetings, although they did not attach much value to their membership beyond its utility. Some people argued that political parties were not that important beyond gaining access to land or farm inputs; such people viewed attending political gatherings as detrimental to their farm activities. Below I provide a summary of biographies gathered during fieldwork which demonstrates the instrumentality of ZANU PF membership during the land reform:

Mr Sibanda was a former soldier in the Zimbabwe's national army; he retired from the army in 2005. He was stationed in Bulawayo where he owned a house in the Mpopoma Township. After retirement, he wanted to start farming and thus was allocated an A1 plot at Damvuri:

> I am originally from Mhondoro Ngezi although I lived in Bulawayo where I worked and own a house. My brother organised a plot for me here. I came in 2003, and was offered a plot in village 8. As a former member of the army, I was given a plot because I am a war veteran. However, I was not necessarily a member of ZANU PF although I registered and carry a card. In 2006, I ran into trouble for not attending ZANU PF meetings, many people suspected me of not supporting ZANU PF, the DA threatened to evict me from the plot if I did not proof my commitment to ZANU PF. I went to the DA and argued that no one could question my party credentials, I fought in the DRC war and went to war during the armed struggle. I successfully defended myself although I am not really a supporter of ZANU PF. As a soldier I support the land reform but I don't support ZANU PF, I just carry a card for political protection. (interviewed at Damvuri on 23/10/2010)

Mr Chimuti came from Gokwe in 2003; he and another group of land seekers came through the DA's office in Kadoma. He was allocated a plot at Village 3:

> I came from Gokwe where I was born, we heard about the availability of land in Kadoma and decided to come here. We were brought here by the army, at that time of jambanja,[3] one needed to be ZANU PF to

---

[3] Jambanja means violence.

gain access to land. Since we were land seekers, we made sure that we had our ZANU PF membership cards. I had never been a member of ZANU PF but through the land reform I joined. In fact, I would say that all people who joined jambanja became members. But don't get me wrong, being a genuine member is another question altogether. I joined because I wanted land. The question of being a genuine member or not is irrelevant. As long as I have land I don't care about political parties. (interviewed at Damvuri on 23/10/2010)

Mr Mhande came from the town of Kadoma near Danvuri. He used to work for the state-owned electricity company as a meter reader. In 2000, he was allocated a plot at Village 7:

I used to work for the government. We were the first people to come here. We forced the white farmer to move from this farm and were involved in pegging the plots before the government came to officialise them. Everyone here is ZANU PF but not in the sense of being die hard supporters. It's a practical decision to be ZANU PF. We do not necessarily agree with everything ZANU PF does, we support ZANU PF because it gave us land and farming inputs. Although one can say everybody is ZANU PF here, this does not mean there are no people who support other political parties. For example, our local councillor is known to be an MDC supporter but is a ZANU PF councillor. This means that even MDC people carry ZANU PF cards and hold positions in ZANU PF structures. Besides how do you prove if a person is ZANU PF or not? If you carry a card and attend meetings you are ZANU PF even if you are MDC. (interviewed at Damvuri on 24/10/2010)

The biographies provided above demonstrate peasant agency in manipulating political party identities to gain access to land. However, they also show how problematic it is to place people in rigid political categories. People viewed ZANU PF membership as instrumental to their needs as new farmers. They used such membership to access land, farming inputs and other livelihood opportunities. Membership of ZANU PF cannot be taken for granted as it was often 'performed'. Furthermore, interviews with informants show that land beneficiaries cannot be depicted as passive clients of a patrimonial state, as such people actively 'resisted' and manipulated political party membership to their benefit. As the next section will show, peasant agency went beyond faking ZANU PF membership; it also involved other forms of invisible resistance which are explored in detail below.

'Every Day Forms of Resistance' after the Land Reform

In Mhondoro Ngezi, people resettled at the former Damvuri conservancy were allocated land under the A1 model scheme (villagized); although the model was designed to separate crop fields and common grazing lands, the boundaries imposed by technocrats during land demarcation processes have become fluid and are being continuously reshaped by the newly resettled farmers. Acts of resistance against land use plans imposed by the state are reflected in the way people have been able to illegally extend their plots into areas that were technically designated as common grazing lands. Moreover, some people have 'sidetracked' from official land use plans by moving their homesteads from designated areas to crop fields. Their rationale for moving homesteads to their 'fields' was that they wanted to guard their crops from baboons and warthogs which normally invade crop fields in the night and early hours of the morning. However, by moving to their crop fields, such people have become 'invisible' and thus difficult to police.

However, it seems the reshaping of the land use plans by ordinary people reflects ongoing resistance against the new tenure regime imposed by the state during the planning phase of the land reform. Such people tend to disregard officially pegged boundaries since they see them as open to negotiation. The absence of fences between individual plots and common lands means that boundaries can be easily ignored or manipulated.

Take for example Arthur Manaka who came from the nearby Mhondoro Ngezi CA and works at a small-scale gold mine near Damvuri. He had been able to use his wages to expand his agricultural operations by extending his plot into common lands without the approval of local authorities. He explained his strategy by stating:

> I was very lucky to get a plot bordering the common grazing lands. This means when the need arises, I will simply take more land since nobody owns these grazing areas. The good part of getting land here is that unlike in communal areas there is so much land that if one is a hard worker one can put as much land under the plough as possible. (interviewed on 12/02/2011)

Another informant, Thimba, observed how he has extended his yard beyond the one hectare he was given.

> I have been able to extend my yard beyond the 2 acres that I was allocated. Officially, we are not supposed to use the yard for agricultural purposes but for orchards. We have 10 hectare plots located further away

from here. However, I have extended my orchard into common grazing land and I am growing crops rather that fruit trees. I have also taken a large part of land belonging to my neighbor as he was not extending his own yard. (interviewed at Damvuri on 15/05/2011)

The above interviews show how land use plans and plot boundaries imposed by technocrats are being ignored or manipulated by land beneficiaries. It also shows that, post the land reform, there is flexibility over plot sizes as the removal of fences has made it possible for people to illegally extend their plots beyond official demarcations by government technocrats. However, this is likely to lead to conflicts over grazing land that is running out due to ongoing encroachment.

It is not only ordinary people who have disobeyed land use plans dictated by the new tenure regime. Representatives of local authority structures such as village heads, village development committees (VIDCOs), councillors and local ZANU PF leaders have also resisted state-imposed cadastral processes which they are meant to police. Interviews with key informants such as war veteran leaders and village heads indicate that a new village was illegally carved out of state land that had been left as common grazing land by technocrats from government. This village was created to accommodate sons of land benefi-ciaries and 'squatters' who did not benefit from the initial land allocations. The village remains 'illegal' since it has not been registered with the lands ministry. During an interview, the VIDCO chairman explained to me why they created a village without government approval.

We decided to create a village for our sons. Remember during the land reform, it was only the parents who got land. The plots we were given are not big enough to accommodate our sons who are now married. We decided to go ahead and allocate them land before advising relevant authorities of our decision. There is nothing wrong with what we did, we need to look out for our sons before the land runs out. After all this land belongs to us as it was left for grazing our livestock. (interviewed at Damvuri on 15/05/2011)

The above demonstrates the agency of newly resettled farmers in terms of their ability to 'side track' from the official land allocation process as a way of safeguarding their livelihoods. Another form of resistance to the state-imposed tenure regime has been the gradual increase in people utilizing so-called ver-nacular land markets (Chimhowu and Woodhouse 2005) to access land. Interviews with informants show that customary authorities and other local elites are involved in the illegal sale of land. A case in point is that of a local chief who has reportedly subdivided an A2 farm he was allocated by the government into five-hectare plots for resale to land seekers. According to informants, the chief charged somewhere between US$300 and US$700 for a five-hectare plot. However, the chief is reported to have told his clients that they were not paying for the land but that payment was for what is locally known as *chiuchiro chamambo* (a token of appreciation) for being allocated land by a *mambo* (chief) or *muridzi wevhu* (owner of the soil). Interviews recorded during fieldwork below provide a snapshot of how informal land markets are unfolding in Mhondoro Ngezi:

> When my father was allocated land in 2000, he had many sons that did not benefit from the land reform. My four brothers and I are now married but we do not have land. Our father's 10 ha plot is too small to accommodate all of us. Although one of my brothers have been allocated land in a newly opened up village, I was not able to secure a plot. I was forced to go and approach a chief nearby who had subdivided his A2 farm into A1 plots and selling them to land seekers. I paid five hundred dollars (US$ 500) to secure a 5 ha plot. (Manjoro interviewed at Damvuri on 20/09/2014)

Another informant came all the way from Harare to buy a plot after a relative of his told him that a local chief was selling land as he had not benefited from the land reform:

> I did not benefit from the land reform as I did not join land occupations or apply for land. I decided that I could just buy a plot from a chief who I was told was selling land. I still live in the city in Harare but would one day want to retire to my plot. I paid US$700 dollars but the chief is taking time to allocate me the plot I paid for. The chief claims I am not paying for the land, but that payment is a token fee for being shown a plot by a chief who owns the land. (Changara interviewed in Harare on 13/11/2014)

The above shows that informal land markets are increasingly becoming an important avenue for the landless to access land. There are two important reasons for the above. First, as noted in the interviews above, under the fast track land reforms, a household was allocated one plot regardless of the land needs of the sons of beneficiaries who are now married and in need of their own land. This has forced such landless sons to resort to informal land markets as they cannot access the land through official channels. Second, since not everyone benefited from the land reform, those who did not join the land occupations and hence did not gain access to land are now forced to utilize informal land markets as they cannot access land through formal channels. This shows that land reform is not a finished business, and that struggles over land are likely to remain for the foreseeable future. Recent pronouncements by the minster of lands that 'the fast track land reform was officially over' (*Zimbabwe Herald Newspaper*, 8 February 2016) are likely to lead to the intensification of informal land markets as official channels are now closed. So-called vernacular land markets are thus increasingly becoming an important pathway for the landless to access land. Such markets must thus be conceptualized as both a form of peasant agency and resistance to state-making processes during a changing agrarian situation; this is often ignored in literature. Another important point to highlight here is that the fast track land reform has created an atmosphere of flexibility in land tenure which has allowed landless people to access land and through informal means. This flexibility in tenure extends to the utilization of natural resources formally enclosed under the previous agrarian structure. I have explored in detail elsewhere (Mkodzongi 2016) how peasants have taken advantage of the land reform to illegally extract natural resources. This is especially the case for artisanal mining activities which have dramatically increased post the land reforms.

The Mhondoro Ngezi case study demonstrates that peasants deploy various strategies to access land and other livelihood opportunities associated with the land reform. They also resist state-imposed tenure regimes which they often manipulate to suit their local needs. For such people, membership of the ZANU PF political party is seen as instrumental to one's survival. People are more concerned about protecting their land and accessing government help than belonging to political parties. Although they participate in ZANU PF meetings, this is seen as a means to an end. Furthermore, people view the new land tenure regime as flexible, allowing them to either extend their plots beyond the boundaries imposed by technocrats during the land demarcation process or to participate in informal land markets to access land. This shows that peasants are not passive clients of a patrimonial state but active participants in a changing agrarian situation.

The above shows that although people joined ZANU PF under pressure and attend meetings, such people have agency to manipulate such membership for their own survival. Debates about how people accessed land and their association with ZANU PF during the fast track reforms must take into consideration the agency of land seekers in terms of their strategies of accessing land and how such land is utilized beyond the state conceptualization of tenure as prescribed in the 'official' offer letter.

Conclusion

This chapter has demonstrated that peasants were not passive beneficiaries of state patronage during the implementation of Zimbabwe's fast track land reforms. It shows that peasants were active participants in a changing agrarian situation who deployed 'weapons of the weak' to access land and other livelihoods opportunities. Peasant agency involved inter alia, faking political party identities, illegally extending plots and creation of new villages beyond the ones demarcated by government officials. This local experience challenges claims that beneficiaries of the land reform were 'passive' clients of a patrimonial state'.

Chapter 4

GOVERNING THE LAND AFTER THE LAND REFORM

One of the major criticisms of Zimbabwe's fast track land reform programme (FTLRP) was that it led to the 'unravelling' of local state institutions (Hammar 2003; Alexander 2006). Political events that characterized the watershed moments of 2000 when land occupations took place across the Zimbabwean countryside were captured in apocalyptic terms. It was claimed that the violence witnessed across the Zimbabwean countryside during the land occupations signified the end of 'modernity' and that Zimbabwe had entered a fascist cycle (Scarnecchia 2006; Worby 2003). A discourse centred on state collapse which was largely influenced by the media representation of the land reform process emerged. This discourse acquired currency in academia, especially during the *jambanja* phase of land reform, and influenced the way in which Zimbabwe's changing agrarian structure was conceptualized (Hammar et al. 2003). Competing arguments about the dynamics of land occupations and their impact on local state structures also polarized academia (Hammar et al. 2003; Moyo and Yeros 2005; Mamdani 2008; Scarnecchia et al. 2008). However, these arguments were undermined by the absence of empirical data to support them as well as counter claims. The increase in fieldwork-driven studies during the so-called planning phase of land reform after 2004 provided the much-needed evidence on the outcomes of land reform and the way it had an impact on rural governance (Moyo and Yeros 2005; Moyo et al. 2009; Scoones et al. 2010, 2012; Matondi 2012).

Data from these studies suggest that the FTLRP fundamentally transformed rural authority structures. During the onset of land occupations in 2000, chiefs and war veterans who led them emerged as prominent actors in the rural polity with some authority over land. Local state structures such as Village Development Committees (VIDCOs), Ward Development Committees (WADCOs) and District Administrators (DAs) had to contend with having to share their role over rural administration with war veterans and chiefs who in some places had become powerful political figures. In the aftermath of land reform, the emergence of actors such as war veterans in the new authority structures has had a bearing in the way authority over land is claimed and exercised by diverse actors, both state and non-state. State making in the context of Zimbabwe's agrarian reform has thus been shaped by competing claims of authority over land as land occupations 'marked a transformation of the state and political sphere' (Alexander 2006: 187). But how does the rural authority structure look like more than a decade after the implementation of fast track land reform? What are the dynamics of the multiforms of authority that have emerged in the aftermath of the land reform? How do ordinary people engage with these new structures of authority? This chapter aims to highlight how authority over the countryside has changed in the aftermath of land reform. It explores the way in which the state, war veterans, chiefs and ZANU PF structures compete to claim authority over the countryside. The chapter also highlights how newly resettled people engage with the new structures of authority.

Land Occupations and the Transformation of Rural Authority

The way land occupations unfolded across the Zimbabwean countryside meant that its outcomes have retained a localized character. The way in which various actors such as war veterans, chiefs and ZANU PF activists could claim authority over land during land occupations was contested and negotiated, not a straightforward winner takes all scenario as has been suggested by some scholars (Alexander 2003; Hammar 2003). Although in many areas state authority was certainly challenged by war veterans and ZANU PF activists, especially during *jambanja*, political circumstances that obtained across the countryside did not allow a total collapse of local state institutions as often claimed by critics of land reform. There is evidence (Moyo and Yeros 2007; Moyo et al. 2009; Scoones et al. 2010) to suggest that the influence of war veterans during the land occupations varied from one place to the other and that class and ethno-regional dynamics influenced the process of land occupations and subsequent redistribution. In some places (Chaumba et al. 2003), war veterans had a free reign to take control over the redistribution of occupied farms, especially during the *jambanja* phase. However, in other places such as Mhondoro Ngezi, for example, local state structures remained in charge of the land reform with war veterans being reduced to providing logistical support during the redistribution of occupied farms. Claims that during land reform 'ministries charged with agrarian policy were marginalised in favour of an alliance led by ZANU PF and war veterans' (Alexander 2006: 187), and that local state structures were 'unravelled' (Hammar 2003), are problematic and do not sufficiently capture the shifting alliances and the dynamics of authority in the countryside during the land occupations.

Far from being totally overrun and undermined by ZANU PF and war veterans, empirical data gathered in Mhondoro has demonstrated that the state was 'present' in the countryside, although in some places its presence was 'spatial'. Moyo and Yeros (2005) have highlighted how when land reform entered the planning phase the state gradually assumed a hegemonic role over the land reform process and the rural polity at large. However, given the wider political context which obtained from 2004 onwards, the state had to contend with sharing the political space with war veterans and chiefs given their strategic importance in the countryside, especially during the elections. Chapters 2 and 3 highlight how bureaucrats in Mhondoro Ngezi had an upper hand over land redistribution rather than war veterans. As the leader of the local District Lands Committee (DLC), the DA based in Kadoma was able to challenge attempts by the war veterans to lead the land redistribution and resettlement exercise. Land redistribution in Mhondoro Ngezi thus followed a rather technocratic trajectory from the start, reflecting the influence of state structures. During the land reform, bureaucrats instrumentalized their leadership positions in DLCs and their influence in ZANU PF patronage networks to leverage control over land redistribution.

In their study of the outcomes of the fast track land reforms, Moyo and Yeros (2005: 189) have highlighted how during the planning phase of land reform 'bureaucrats sought to develop hegemony over land occupations' through their 'control of the ideological content of media presentations of the third *chimurenga*'. This demonstrates that initially the state suffered setbacks in exercising its authority, especially from 2000 when war veterans and chiefs led land occupations across the countryside until 2004 when the land reform entered the planning phase. However, it soon sought to reassert its authority across the newly resettled areas where war veterans and chiefs had in some places assumed hegemony over the newly resettled areas. This process resulted in contested claims of authority over land.

In order to provide a historical context to the dynamic shifts in rural authority which were occasioned by the fast track land reform process in 2000, it is necessary to briefly rewind to the earlier period immediately after independence. Alexander (2006) has highlighted how state making after independence in 1980 entailed attempts to replace customary authorities with democratic bureaucratic structures such as VIDCOs, WADCOs and Rural District Councils (RDCs). Similarly, Drinkwater (1989: 288) has highlighted how a centralized bureaucracy was 'the most important legacy of the colonial period' and that there are 'continuities between contemporary land use policies and those of technical development phase of the 1920s and 1960s'. This legacy is demonstrated by the way state making and rural administration were conceptualized after independence (Herbst 1990; Munro 1998). A key policy feature of rural administration after independence was the promulgation of laws which sought to curtail customary authority in favour of the so-called democratic local governance structures epitomized by newly created RDCs. According to Moyo et al.,

> Zimbabwe's local government system had evolved since independence to an extent that traditional leadership structures in the communal areas had lost their land allocating powers to District Councils. In practice the passing of the Communal Land Act (1982) did not have any significant impact on the role of traditional authorities as people in the communal areas continued to recognise traditional authorities in terms of their land allocation and dispute settlement responsibilities. The Rural District Councils (responsible for LSCF areas) and the District Councils responsible for CAs were in 1988 amalgamated through the Rural District Councils Act, with traditional leaders being subordinated more effectively under RDCs. The RDC is composed of elected ward representatives (councillors) and a chief executive officer who is responsible for the daily operations of the council. (2009: 146)

This means that in theory chiefs who were historically an important pillar of colonial rural administration were subordinated to RDCs and politically sidelined by the 'modernizing' tendencies of the postcolonial state. However, in practice customary authority remained intact as people in the countryside continued to recognize the land allocation powers of chiefs (Moyo et al. 2009).

The onset of land occupations in 2000 further emboldened customary authority as chiefs became dominant political actors in the countryside due to their role in leading the land occupations. Unlike before when bureaucrats reigned supreme in the countryside, state making in the context of fast track land reform had to be based on the co-option of chiefs and war veterans who had become prominent political actors in the countryside. War veterans and chiefs played an influential role in rural areas as members of DLCs who were responsible for local land allocation processes during the implementation of the FTLRP. These local actors became a key part of the local 'state' alongside VIDCOs and WADCOs, although their influence varied from one place to the other. However, it is important to highlight here that although chiefs and war veterans emerged as dominant political actors during and after land reform, their authority and influence have fluctuated significantly, from playing a hegemonic role during the *jambanja* phase to working under the state after 2004 when the land reform entered its planning phase. The relationship between the state and these local actors cannot be simplified as it is largely influenced by local political dynamics. The influence and authority of chiefs and war veterans varies from one place to the other and so does their utility. In some places, the land reform weakened customary authority while in other places chiefs have become powerful actors in the rural polity due to their ability to deploy ancestral autochthony to make claims over 'ancestral' lands (Mujere 2011).

In the context of Zimbabwe's FTLRP, a better understanding of how authority in the countryside is claimed and exercised by the state and the local actors (such as chiefs and war veterans) requires that we move away from simplifying the way in which local authority structures operate and how different actors claim authority. It is also important to conceptualize state making during the land reform as a contested process involving a diversity of actors both state and non-state. Moreover, it is also important to disaggregate individual authority structures in order to unmask class and ethno-regional dynamics which influence the way they operate. For example, discourses of belonging in Mhondoro Ngezi have shaped the way chiefs and ZANU PF structures operate in terms of the ability of individuals within these organizations to contest for political positions. Such discourses have also shaped the way ordinary people view such authority structures in terms of their legitimacy. The next section analyses how chiefs and ZANU PF interface with the state in the dynamics of rural authority in the aftermath of the land reform process.

The Role of ZANU PF in Local Governance

ZANU PF political party structures were instrumental in the way the FTLRP was implemented. In conjunction with war veterans, ZANU PF activists mobilized the peasantry and were central in the way the white-owned farms were occupied and how such occupations were legitimized. Chapter 3 highlighted how peasants utilized ZANU PF structures to access the land. In the aftermath of land reform, ZANU PF structures have remained a key part of the rural authority structure. Interviews with resettled people in Mhondoro Ngezi indicated that local ZANU PF networks are central in the way resettled people gain access to patronage networks. For example, access to government assistance such as farming inputs which are critical for resettled farmers is negotiated through ZANU PF structures.

Moreover, employment at the South African-owned Zimbabwe Platinum Mines (ZIMPLATS) which is located in the area is negotiated through ZANU PF structures. An informant highlighted how the ZIMPLATS mine operates a 'ZANU PF' quota system in its recruitment as a way of buying political protection. The informant claimed that for local people to be employed at ZIMPLATS, their names must be on a list which is usually kept by local chiefs or the local Member of Parliament (MP). The list is periodically handed over to ZIMPLATS management when employment opportunities arise. The mine will then invite the persons on the list for an interview just as a formality, as they would have already secured employment by virtue of their ZANU PF connections. Those whose names are not on the list face challenges in being employed at the mine despite the fact that the mine has an official policy of employing local people based on merit (interview with Mhuru at Damvuri on 28/10/2011). ZIMPLATS also operates a wide range of corporate social responsibility programmes such as building new schools and supporting local communities with financial resources to build or repair clinics and schools. However, informants claimed that such programmes are sometimes manipulated by local ZANU PF politicians for personal gain (interview with Chiwaro at Damvuri on 23/10/2011). It is this instrumentality of ZANU PF patronage networks that makes it central in the way resettled people survive in a largely difficult socio-economic environment.

However, the way ZANU PF patronage networks operate is complex and is influenced by diverse factors such as ethnicity, class and ongoing intra-factional politics. The relationship between ordinary people and ZANU PF structures is dynamic and influenced by prevailing factional politics pitting ZANU PF politicians against each other. These factional struggles have to some extent influenced the demographic composition of land beneficiaries at the former Damvuri conservancy. Factional struggles also continue to shape the way in which local structures of authority operate and how individuals bid for leadership positions in local authority structures such as VIDCOs and WADCOs.

Interviews with informants indicate that ethnicity influenced the way one could access ZANU PF patronage structures. It was also influential in the way individuals could bid for political positions within ZANU PF. For example, contested claims of belonging have emerged after resettlement at the Damvuri conservancy with various groups claiming to be the genuine 'autochthons' while disqualifying others who have become perceived as 'strangers'. These groups constitute people who originally came from the nearby Mhondoro Ngezi CA and those from Gokwe. During the interviews, informants in the Mhondoro Ngezi CA group claimed that people from Gokwe were brought to the area by Paul Mangwana, a ZANU PF politician who was the MP for the Mhondoro Ngezi constituency at the onset of land occupations in 2000. Mangwana is originally from Masvingo Province where the *Karanga* ethnic group predominates (Karanga is a dialect of the Shona language). Informants in the Mhondoro Ngezi CA group claimed that during his tenure as MP for the Mhondoro Ngezi constituency, Mangwana utilized his political influence and connections with the local DA in Kadoma to secure land for people from Gokwe and Sanyati areas who largely belong to his 'Karanga' ethnic group.

According to these claims, the main reason for this was that he sought to dilute the influence of local *Zezuru* ethnic groups (another dialect of the Shona language) which he suspected of supporting Bright Matonga, a rival former ZANU PF politician. Matonga comes from the local area and belongs to the Zezuru ethnic group which predominates in the Mhondoro Ngezi area (interview with Musvusvudzi at Damvuri on 24/09/2010).

Informants in the Mhondoro Ngezi CA group, who are largely from the *Zezuru* ethnic group, expressed some resentment towards Mangwana and the people from Gokwe whom they perceive as being 'outsiders' from another part of the country. While people in the Gokwe group perceived as being 'strangers' have argued against such perceptions and labels, they claimed that the main reason they came to the Mhondoro Ngezi District during land occupations was their historical connection with the area. They claim to be part of a group of people who were forcibly removed from the former Rhodesdale crown lands by the colonial government in the 1950s and resettled in Sanyati and Gokwe. Land reform had created an opportunity for them to recover their ancestral land lost during the colonial era (interview with Lozane at Damvuri on 23/10/2011). During interviews, people originally from Gokwe have argued that the *Karanga* identity attached to them was a case of mistaken identity. They claimed that although they spoke the *Karanga* dialect of Shona, they were in fact *Zezurus* who had undergone a linguistic transformation while in Gokwe where they had been forcibly resettled among a large group of Karanga speakers from Masvingo who also had been forcibly relocated to Gokwe in the 1950s (interview with Sibanda at Damvuri on 19/11/2010).

Interviews with informants from both groups indicate that people were divided between those who supported Mangwana and those who supported Matonga based on ethnicity. However, it is difficult to verify to what extent ethnicity had influenced the demographic make-up of the land beneficiaries at the former Damvuri conservancy despite the ethnic dynamics reflected above. A major complicating factor is the localized histories of migration and forced removals dating back to the colonial era which have reshaped people's ethnic identities. A large part of the broader Mhondoro Ngezi area consists of mining and large-scale commercial farms (LSCF). Historically, migration across farms, mines and communal areas was a 'key feature of life' (Spierenburg 2004). Moreover, the forced removals of a large number of Africans from the area in the 1950s (Nyambara 2005) to the low-lying areas of Gokwe further complicated the situation. Some of the people who were forcibly relocated to Gokwe came back to reclaim their 'ancestral lands' through fast track land reform. Given these histories of colonial forced removals and voluntary migrations, it has become 'difficult to make a distinction between immigrants and "autochthons"' (Spierenburg 2004).

What is, however, important is that competing claims of 'belonging' in Mhondoro Ngezi reflect how the newly resettled people seek to legitimize their claims over land and access to ZANU PF patronage structures. For example, the resentment expressed by people in the Mhondoro Ngezi CA group towards those in the Gokwe group stems from the fact that those in the latter group tend to hold key positions of authority in local decision-making structures such as ZANU PF local committees, war veteran structures and VIDCOs. This is despite the fact that people in this group came from areas perceived to be furthest from the Mhondoro Ngezi District. Those in the Mhondoro Ngezi group feel that they have a weak bargaining power over access to resources such as farming inputs and other government assistance due to the fact that they are underrepresented in structures of authority (interview with Chari at Damvuri on 23/11/2010).

Contested claims of belonging between the two groups were also entangled with prevailing intra-ZANU PF factional struggles involving two politicians. People in the Mhondoro group claimed they voted Mangwana out during the 2005 parliamentary elections in favour of Matonga because the later came from the local area (interview with Mrs Muriro at Damvuri on 23/12/2010). Matonga's family belongs to the Benhura chieftaincy which is based in the Mhondoro Ngezi CA and thus shares kinship ties with people in the Mhondoro Ngezi CA group. During the 2005 ZANU PF primary elections, Matonga is believed to have utilized his family networks to secure votes before the general election. During his campaign, he went on a road show across the Mhondoro Ngezi constituency accompanied by elders from the Benhura chieftaincy. A crucial part of the tour involved being introduced to all the chieftaincies across the Mhondoro Ngezi constituency such as Chiefs Nyika, Mushava and Murambwa. He is believed to have lobbied such chiefs to mobilize their subjects in support of him instead of Mangwana who was a 'stranger' from another part of the country. The conflict between the two politicians was resolved after Mangwana lost his parliamentary seat to Matonga and was thus forced to contest for a constituency based in his native Chivi area in Masvingo Province (interview with Chikava at Damvuri on 13/10/2010).

A complicating factor to these autochthonic-based ZANU PF factional struggles emerged when the Mhondoro Ngezi constituency was delineated before the 2008 harmonized elections. The delineation resulted in the creation of the Muzvezve constituency covering the newly resettled former LSCF areas and the Mhondoro Ngezi constituency comprising old resettlement areas and the Mhondoro Ngezi CA. In the 2008 harmonized elections, the newly created Muzvezve constituency was won by Peter Haritatos, a white farmer and ZANU PF politician based in the nearby town of Kadoma. While many white land owners across the area lost their land during the land occupations,

Haritatos, who is an ardent ZANU PF supporter, kept his farm and became an MP of a constituency carved out of largely former white-owned LSCFs which were resettled through fast track land reform. Interviews with his constituent members indicate that he is a very popular politician despite being a white farmer. This contradicts the general anti-white farmer political rhetoric popularized by senior ZANU PF politicians, including Mugabe. Informants at Damvuri praised Haritatos for supporting the development of the newly resettled area and for periodically donating seeds and farming inputs to local people. Above all, he is believed to be less corrupt than other ZANU PF political elites such as Mangwana whom they voted out because of corruption and negligence (interview with Mututudzi at Damvuri on 23/08/2010).

It was difficult to know why people thought Haritatos was less corrupt even though it seemed he had also instrumentalized ZANU PF patronage structures as a way of gathering votes during his political campaigns. Like many ZANU PF politicians, Haritatos also deployed belonging and his participation in the liberation struggle as a way of legitimizing his right to represent the local area in parliament:

> I am a son of the soil. I was born in this area although I am of Greek origin. During the Rhodesia times, Greek people were regarded as blacks, we were not allowed in white private schools. I remember as a young man I was barred from attending a white private school in Kadoma. We suffered a lot of racism during the Rhodesia time. I joined ZANU PF during the liberation struggle because of my experience during the colonial times. The Rhodesians were racist and it was right that we took land from them. During the land occupations I told the President that I wanted to give up my farm for redistribution. However, the President said I should keep the farm because that was my pension. The President supported me and appointed me to the senate until I became an MP for the Muzvezve Constituency in 2008. I am grooming my son to understand the struggle. He is now in the Mashonaland West provincial executive. (interviewed in Zvimba North on 25/08/2013)

This highlights the way 'belonging' is deployed by various people within ZANU PF regardless of their race. Despite Haritatos's 'whiteness', his family has a long history of farming in the area and participation in the liberation struggle. He speaks fluent Shona and thus 'belongs' to the Mhondoro Ngezi area. Most local people address him affectionately as 'Baba vaGeorge' (George's father), a Shona way of addressing people by their first born child's name (interview with Nyati at Damvuri on 10/06/2010). This highlights the ambiguities associated with claims of 'belonging' in the way they are instrumentalized by various individuals and groups aligned to the ZANU PF political party. Although Haritatos's case is unique given the general anti-white rhetoric which underpinned the land occupations, it challenges general assumptions about white farmers being always victims of land reform and the 'foreign' label attached to their identity.

The Mhondoro Ngezi case study shows how discourses of belonging play an important role in the way ordinary people compete to make claims over land and to access ZANU PF patronage networks. Moreover, belonging is also crucial to the way ZANU PF politicians bid for political office. Autochthonic struggles have thus shaped the way individuals in ZANU PF bid for political power. These struggles reflect a 'differentiated politics and strategies of belonging – from "below" as well as from "above" ' (Christiansen and Hedetoft 2004). Overall, the above demonstrates that the way ZANU PF functions is dynamic and is prone to prevailing ethnic-based factional struggles.

The Dynamics of Customary Authority after the Land Reform

One of the major outcomes of fast track land reform was the opening up of former LSCF areas to customary authority. As highlighted earlier, the chiefs were important political actors during the land occupations due to their role in mobilizing the peasantry. Within the post-fast track land reform era, chiefs have emerged as a key part of the rural polity with some authority over land. The role of chiefs in rural administration has gone through dynamic changes which are worth examining in order to understand their current role in relation to land reform. The postcolonial state-making process entailed attempts to subordinate chiefs to RDCs as the government sought to dilute their authority. Under the Ministry of Local Government Urban and Rural Development Act (1982), customary authority was limited to communal areas (formerly reserves), while newly created resettlement areas and rural councils (formerly responsible for LSCF areas) were outside their jurisdiction. However, attempts by the post-independence political regime to sideline chiefs in rural administration were largely unsuccessful as they continued to dominate rural administration, controlling access to land despite such powers having been transferred to RDCs (Herbst 1990; Munro 1998; Alexander 2006). Customary authority was consolidated in the late 1990s when 'there was an apparent shift in Government thinking in 1999 as traditional leaders were once again upgraded to the status of salaried civil servants through the Traditional Leaders Act' (Moyo et al. 2009: 147). The onset of fast track land reform and changes in laws governing rural administration meant that chiefs became an important part of rural administration. The onset of land occupations allowed them to extend their jurisdiction over former LSCF resettled under fast track land

reform. In the aftermath of land reform, chiefs have sought to deploy ancestral autochthony as a way of extending their influence and authority over
newly resettled territories. In his study based in the Gutu area, in the south of
Zimbabwe, Mujere highlighted how

> FTLRP has thus provided traditional authorities with an opportunity to
> pursue an agenda akin to land restitution as they have been making a
> number of claims both substantiated and unsubstantiated over the new
> settlements which they regard as their *Matongo* (old homes). (2011: 7)

In Mhondoro Ngezi, three chiefs (Nyika, Benhura and Ngezi) based in the
nearby Mhondoro Ngezi CA took advantage of the land reform to recast
their authority over 'ancestral lands' opened up during fast track land reform.
However, despite having made territorial claims over newly resettled territories, most of the chiefs have remained in the CA except for Chief Nyika
who acquired an A2 plot (commercial farm) at the Rock bar Ranch to the
south of Damvuri. Despite having a second home at his newly acquired farm,
Chief Nyika maintained his communal area homestead and now straddles
between the two locations holding court sessions at both places. However,
Chiefs Benhura and Ngezi did not acquire any land in the new areas and
have remained in CAs, although they both made territorial claims over the
new resettled areas. Both chiefs have devised creative ways of demonstrating
'effective' rule' or 'beneficial occupation' (James 2006). Chief Benhura is
believed to have informally appointed his uncle who was allocated land at
the former Damvuri conservancy to act as a headman while Chief Ngezi has
sought to validate his territorial claims through periodic visits to the newly
resettled area to 'familiarize' himself with his new territory and subjects.
    In 1999, just before the onset of the land occupations, Chief Ngezi caused
some controversy when he was reported to have conducted a spiritual cleansing
ceremony at the future site of the ZIMPLATS mine. According to informants,
the ritual was a way of seeking the approval of local Mhondoro royal ancestral spirits before the mining company could start its mining operations. He
claimed that his ancestors were buried in the Mulota Hills where the mine
intended to start its platinum mining operations. According to reports which
appeared in the local media, the chief conducted a ritual at the site of his
ancestral graves by the *chemakudo* shrine in order to avoid 'the wrath of the
ancestors in the Mulota Hills'.
    However, the ritual became a source of conflict because of contested claims
over the ownership of the territory where the mine is located. Both Chiefs
Nyika and Benhura who have also made claims over the area are reported
to have boycotted the ritual which they dismissed as a political ploy by Chief

Ngezi to prejudice them of their ancestral lands. They are believed to have argued that as a 'stranger', Chief Ngezi's ancestors had no legitimate claim over the area where the mine is located and hence no spiritual power to cause accidents at the mine. They further argued that cleansing rituals can only be undertaken by representatives of the genuine *Mhondoro* spirits (interview with Chief Benhura at Manyewe on 25/04/2010). These contested claims over the new territories continue to be a source of conflicts and the mine has become a site of autochthonic struggles.

Historically, the boundaries among the three chieftaincies are loosely based on two rivers (Mungezi and Muzvezve) which both flow westwards from the Mhondoro Ngezi CAs towards the contested territories. Chief Nyika's territory is located to the south of the Mungezi River which forms a boundary with Chief Benhura's territory. Chief Benhura's territory is located between Mungezi River to the south and Muzvezve River to the north. Chief Ngezi's territory is located to the north of the Muzvezve River. However, the major problem is that since these chiefs had no jurisdiction over the newly resettled areas before 2000, claims of ownership of such territories are difficult to authenticate. Moreover, histories of colonial land alienation and forced removals meant that boundaries between chieftaincies have constantly changed as more land was alienated for European use (Nyambara 2005).

Interviews with the three chiefs demonstrate the problematic nature of claims over ancestral lands which have emerged in the aftermath of land reform. Histories of colonial forced removals mean that the ownership of newly resettled territories and the boundaries between them has significantly changed with time. This makes it difficult to identify the legitimate claimant of the newly resettled territory among the three chiefs. Moreover, claims over the newly resettled areas are problematic if one takes into account archival records. According to Native Commissioner Delineation Reports (National Archives of Zimbabwe file S2929/4/1), all the three chiefs have never historically owned land in the former LSCF areas of Mhondoro Ngezi. These records indicate that such territories historically belonged to Chiefs Muyambi and Chirima who were forcibly relocated to the Gokwe area in the 1940s.

Competing claims over the newly resettled areas among the three chieftaincies have been largely fuelled by the presence of mineral resources such as gold and platinum in the newly resettled areas. Zimbabwe's biggest platinum mine, the South African-owned ZIMPLATS mine, is located in the newly resettled areas by the Mulota Hills near the boundary between the Mhondoro Ngezi CA and the former LSCF areas. In 2012, the company's mining operations became the centre of autochthonic struggles after it agreed to an indigenization package with the Government of Zimbabwe (GoZ). Under Zimbabwe's

Indigenisation and Economic Empowerment Act, public companies are required to cede a 51 per cent stake to indigenous Zimbabweans.

The indigenization of the mine has resulted in conflicts among the chiefs, ordinary people and ZANU PF-aligned political elites. Struggles to gain access to economic opportunities associated with the mine intensified in 2012 after the company agreed to cede a 51 per cent stake to local people in order to comply with Zimbabwe's indigenization laws. The former ZANU PF local MP and other high-profile ZANU PF politicians such as Ignatius Chombo (former minister of local government and rural housing) and Saviour Kasukuwere (former minister of youth and indigenization) contested each other to control access to the trust fund.

On the other hand, local chiefs who claim to be the custodians of the land where the mine is located have protested against elite corruption, arguing that they must be the ones in charge of the trust given the fact that the mine is located in their ancestral lands. What further complicated the situation is that the local chiefs are not in agreement among themselves in terms of who should be in charge. For example, Chief Nyika, who claimed to be the legitimate custodian of the land where the mine is located, threatened to boycott the 'government'-initiated Mhondoro Ngezi Community Share-Ownership Trust (CSOT) in favour of the Mhondoro Community Development Trust which he helped to create. The chief argued that he did not want to be part of a trust initiated by politicians who do not 'belong' to the area. His other major contention was that the late chief Murambwa, whose territory is located further away to the northern part of the Mhondoro Ngezi CA, was appointed by politicians to be the first chair of the CSOT. He accused politicians of sidelining him by appointing an 'outsider' to lead the trust while he as both a 'paramount' chief and the legitimate 'custodian' of the territory where the mine is located was sidelined.

Struggles over the control of the CSOT eventually forced politicians to concede to his demands by agreeing that the chairmanship of the trust should rotate among all the chiefs from the area on an annual basis. This demonstrates the dynamics of authority over land and natural resources which have emerged in the aftermath of land reform. Chief Nyika was forced to abandon his own trust in order to join the one created by politicians, which enjoyed legitimacy from various government departments which are responsible for mineral resource extraction and rural administration. An article in the government-controlled *Sunday Mail* newspaper (8 October 2011) highlighted how chiefs are on one hand able to make claims over land based on ancestral autochthony, but on the other hand such claims can be problematic if they pose a direct threat to state authority over control of land and natural resources:

Chief Nyika was bitter after government recognised the trust chaired by Chief Murambwa instead of his separate initiative known as Mhondoro Community Development Trust [...] However, the government resolved that all chiefs in the district must support the Mhondoro-Ngezi scheme, which President Mugabe is expected to launch on Thursday [...] 'All the chiefs in the area – Murambwa, Mashava, Benhura and Nyika – will be able to lead the development initiative. Chief Murambwa will be the first chair as he is a paramount chief. He is also a member of the Chiefs' Council of Zimbabwe.

This demonstrates that although chiefs have sought to deploy ancestral autochthony to recast their authority over new territories, their claims have largely been undermined by the hegemonic role of the state and local ZANU PF patronage structures. ZANU PF political elites who do not necessarily 'belong' to the local area, such as Saviour Kasukuwere the former minister of the Youth and indigenisation, deployed what Commarof and Commarof (2009) called 'lawfare' as a way of asserting state control of land and what lies below it. During the conflict over the control of the CSOT, local chiefs were reminded of various regulatory frameworks which governed mineral wealth and rural administration and how their claims could only be legitimized if they complied with the law and worked with government. The chiefs were left with limited options but to comply if they wanted to remain politically relevant and to access state patronage structures. This demonstrates the dynamics of state-making processes in the aftermath of fast track land reform. On one hand, chiefs can extend their authority to newly resettled areas, and on the other, such claims are subordinated to state authority and thus must be compliant with relevant laws.

Ordinary people have also protested against elite capture of local resources. For example, indigenization discourses have had an effect of generating 'natural resource activism' across local communities. Discourses of local ownership of natural resources supported by ZANU PF are now emerging from below. Interviews with informants indicate that local communities from the broader Mhondoro Ngezi District are also demanding that the mine should pay back for causing environmental damage to the local area. As a result of such activism, the mine has invested in corporate social responsibility programmes such as building of schools, clinics and repairing of roads as a way of addressing local problems. Moreover, local ZANU PF youths have also lobbied senior politicians to be offered employment at the ZIMPLATS mine as a way accessing the benefits of indigenization. Despite claims of corruption in the way the mine has been 'indigenized', discourses of indigenization have helped ordinary people to challenge political elites and demand access to the benefits of indigenization of the ZIMPLATS mine. Struggles over the control of the Mhondoro Ngezi CSOT reflect the dynamics of state making in the aftermath of land reform. They demonstrate that authority over the countryside is contested and that various actors have utilized diverse mechanisms to legitimize their claims over land and what lies beneath it.

On a different note, although the three chiefs have made territorial claims over newly resettled areas, they have struggled to entrench their authority in newly resettled areas. Interviews with informants in these areas indicate that people are divided in terms of their loyalties to the chiefs. On one hand, former residents of the Mhondoro Ngezi CA tend to support customary authority due to their historical ties with such chiefs with whom they enjoy kinship ties. On the other hand, people who came from places as far as Gokwe and Sanyati with no kinship ties with such chiefs see no reason to submit to their authority. The latter seem to question the authority of chiefs and instead are in favour of local state structures of authority such as the district administrator and rural district councils which they feel better represent their interests.

The legitimacy of chiefs is further weakened by their 'absence' from the newly resettled areas despite having made territorial claims over them. Although the chiefs were part of the local DLC which has control over local land redistribution, they were not actively involved in the land occupations and hence cannot deploy land as an instrument to control the newly resettled people. Unlike in communal areas where they have leverage over their subjects due to their ability to control access to land, they lack such leverage in newly resettled areas where other structures of authority such VIDCOs, WADCOs and ZANU PF structures are heavily involved in controlling access to land. Additionally, contested claims by various chiefs over the new areas have weakened their authority among new communities. It is difficult for people to know which chief is more 'legitimate' among the three. Moreover, the fact that the government has not yet openly endorsed attempts by the chiefs to recast their authority over the new territories makes people question their legitimacy.

There is a general feeling among resettled people, in particular those from Gokwe, that chiefs are associated with communal areas rather than newly resettled areas. Such people view 'resettlement' areas as 'modern' spaces under the authority of government rather than customary authorities. Their attitudes are influenced by the fact that resettlement programmes or *minda mirefu* (long fields) have been historically associated with yeoman farming and perceived 'superior' forms of tenure arrangements better than those obtaining in communal areas. As a result, notions of better tenurial arrangements and superiority of resettlement areas over communal areas persist among newly resettled people. They generally feel that they enjoy a form of 'freehold' tenure as 'new' farmers and thus cannot be answerable to chiefs. The dynamics of authority in Mhondoro Ngezi demonstrate that authority over land in the post-fast track era remains contested among the chiefs and the state. Although political elites instrumentalize customary authority in their state-making projects, they are generally averse to the idea of chiefs wielding too much authority over the countryside. An article in the state-owned *Herald* newspaper (25 January 2012) highlighted the uneasy relationship between chiefs and the state in the aftermath of land reform:

> President Mugabe was speaking at Murombedzi Growth Point to members of the Zvimba chieftainship who were discussing a proposal to create additional chieftainship in the district. He advised the Gushungo clan to resolve the issue amicably in conformity with the Traditional Leaders Act [...] The meeting was aimed at brainstorming on the feasibility of creating more chiefs in Zvimba following geographical transformations spawned by the land reform programme. The area under Chief Zvimba is now too big to effectively administer. The President said it was up to the Gushungo clan to agree on how many chiefs could be added in consultation with the Ministry of Local Government, Rural and Urban Development. He said the chieftainship should not be a source of squabbles.

This exposes the ambiguous relationship between the state and chiefs in the aftermath of land reform. On one hand, chiefs have been afforded a level of leverage to make territorial claims over newly resettled areas while on the other hand, such claims must comply with state patronage processes. Struggles over the proceeds of 'indigenization' reflected by conflicts centred on the indigenization of the ZIMPLATS mine highlight the 'binary antagonisms' (Forster and Koechlin 2011) between local actors and the state in the way patronage networks operate. At local level, contested claims over newly resettled territories among the chiefs highlight the pitfalls of ancestral autochthony in terms of how difficult it is to validate such claims. Overall, it seems the dynamics of authority which underpinned the implementation of the FTLRP have had a profound influence in the way structures of authority operate in the countryside after land reform. State making in the aftermath of land reform entails a dynamic process of negotiation among diverse political actors, both state and non-state. The Mhondoro Ngezi case study explored in this book indicates that although the state has sought to impose a hegemonic presence in the countryside post the land reforms, local actors such as chiefs remain key in the way the state can be embedded in rural society.

Conclusion

This chapter has demonstrated how the fast track land reform process transformed the rural authority structure. In the aftermath of land reform, authority over the countryside is contested between chiefs and the state. The relationship between the state and the chiefs is dynamic and influenced by complex patron–client relationships that are difficult to generalize. The chapter has also highlighted the centrality of ethnicity and belonging in the way newly resettled people compete to access land and ZANU PF patronage networks. Moreover, ethnicity is central in the way political elites compete for political positions. Discourses of 'belonging' are also central to the way chiefs have sought to claim authority over areas that were resettled under the fast track land reform. Discourses of indigenization which have gained some salience in the aftermath of the land reform have had a profound effect on the way authority over land is claimed by both state and chiefs. Chiefs have deployed ancestral autochthony as a way of claiming authority over land and natural resources in the newly resettled areas while political elites have utilized state patronage networks as a way of challenging the legitimacy of chiefly claims over natural resources. In the aftermath of land reform, the relationship between chiefs and the state is dynamic; although the chiefs and the state contest each other in claiming authority over the countryside, chiefs play an important role in the way the state can be embedded in rural society. For example, chiefs are used by the government to mobilize their subject populations in support of government programmes. The ZANU PF political party also utilize chiefs to mobilize their subject communities during elections. This demonstrates that although there are ongoing conflicts between the chiefs and the state, chiefs play an important role in the way the state is embedded in rural society and the way ZANU PF patronage structures operate in the countryside.

Chapter 5

NEW PEOPLE, NEW LAND AND NEW LIVELIHOODS: AN ANALYSIS OF LIVELIHOOD TRAJECTORIES AFTER FAST TRACK LAND REFORM

The outcomes of Zimbabwe's land reform had until recently remained contested. Critics of the fast track land reform process had argued that it resulted in dramatic fall in agricultural productivity (Richardson 2005) and that the new farmers lack the requisite farming skills. However, some scholars, notably Moyo et al. (2009), Scoones et al. (2010) and Hanlon et al. (2012), among others, have highlighted that the land reform was not a total failure as claimed, but that the new farmers are utilizing the land and that some are already accumulating from below. Empirical data gathered in the Mhondoro Ngezi District indicates that the outcomes of the land reform process are more nuanced and require an in-depth understanding of the dynamics that have shaped agricultural investments in the aftermath of land reform. These dynamics were influenced by a wide variety of factors which were often localized in character. To start with, it has been argued that 'the benefits of programs which involve large-scale human resettlement are unlikely to become apparent in less than a generation' (Kinsey and Binswanger 1993), suggesting that it is too early to make generalizations about the success or failure of the new farmers or the fast track land reform programme (FTLRP) at large given the fact that it is little more than a decade since its implementation. Data from the various empirical studies (Moyo et al. 2009; Scoones et al. 2010; Hanlon et al. 2012; Matondi 2012) indicate that a diversity of factors have influenced agricultural investments and land utilization in the aftermath of land reform.

First, the fast track land reform was implemented within a hyperinflationary socio-economic context under which the new farmers had to start from scratch often with very little, and sometimes no, government support in terms of inputs and other social services. Second, the new farmers came from diverse socio-economic backgrounds; some were better endowed with productive resources to utilize the land such as livestock, ploughs, tractors and financial resources to hire labour. Such people were generally able to quickly clear the land and start their farming operations, build homes and hence generally became more successful in their new farming operations. On the other hand, some farmers had limited means to utilize the newly acquired land and hence temporarily sought work in mines in the broader Mhondoro Ngezi area as a way of gaining some income with the hope of investing in their land later.

Since the fast track land reform was a process rather than a one-off event, success in utilizing the land was also dependent on when people were resettled. Those who were resettled in the early stages of land reform around 2000 had better chances of success in making investments on their land. Such people tended to hold positions in local authority structures such as the Committee of Seven, VIDCOs and local ZANU PF (cell or branch) committees. These structures played an important role in the way government assistance in the form of subsidies could be accessed, especially in the early stages of land reform when such inputs were scarce. The people who came later after 2004 during the planning phase generally had limited influence over how vital inputs could be accessed. However, there were those who had their own savings and did not need political connections as they had the resources to invest in their land.

While the situation described above might change in the long term and the new farmers might be better placed to utilize the newly acquired land, there are several questions that we need to answer: What are the new farmers doing with the newly acquired land? What are the new livelihood trajectories that are emerging in the resettled areas? These questions are central to our understanding of what is happening in newly resettled areas in terms of the type of activities shaping livelihoods in the aftermath of land reform.

Utilizing the Land

An important factor to take into consideration when analysing agricultural investments after land reform is the broader socio-economic context which obtained during and after the resettlement. This has a bearing on how and what the new farmers could invest in the newly acquired land. Data from Mhondoro Ngezi indicate that in the aftermath of land reform, agriculture is not the only activity undertaken by the new farmers. Instead, a large number of farmers in Mhondoro Ngezi are also involved in a wide variety of non-farm activities which provide vital sources of income at a time when investing in agriculture has been difficult. Thus, we should not picture the farmers as bonded at farms only involved in agricultural production as that will be misleading. However, investment in non-farm livelihood activities does not constitute a process of de-agrarianization as suggested by some scholars (Bryceson et al. 2000) as the family farm remains a key part of their livelihoods strategies.

In Mhondoro Ngezi, a wide variety of factors influenced the trajectory of agricultural investments after resettlement. 'Success' in utilizing the land was thus highly relative and dependent on many factors, which include, inter alia, the socio-economic background of the farmers and their ability to utilize ZANU PF patronage networks to access agricultural inputs and other support services, which were generally difficult to access. Another important point to consider when analysing agricultural investments after the land reform is that not everyone who acquired land had the aim of immediately utilizing it. Some people, especially those from nearby Mhondoro Ngezi CAs, acquired land as a form of insurance policy for the future given the fact that CAs were congested and ecologically degraded. Such people remained in communal areas where they still enjoy land rights while the newly acquired land has remained underutilized or leased out to other farmers. These factors demonstrate that in any particular context the situation was rather complex and dynamic. Any attempt to make generalizations about the success and failure of the new farmers in utilizing the land must take into account a wide variety of factors which influenced agricultural investments. In their study based in Masvingo, Scoones et al. (2010: 60) utilized a wealth-ranking exercise to construct livelihood typologies. They highlighted 'emerging patterns of social and economic differentiation' among the new farmers. Similar patterns of social and economic differentiation have also been observed in Mhondoro Ngezi and are reflected in the biographies of the new farmers captured in this book.

An analysis of the dynamics of agricultural investments based on selected biographies of the new farmers highlights how patterns of social differentiation influenced success or failure. Some farmers were more successful in making agricultural investments while others have struggled and are thus more involved in off-farm activities such as wage labour and gold panning as they lacked the means to invest in their land. It also highlights that livelihood trajectories after land reform have been dependent on many factors, and that 'a highly complex pattern of livelihood differentiation [...] with hybrid class categories defying any simple ideal type categorisation' (Scoones et al. 2010: 32) has emerged in the aftermath of land reform. The farmers have been loosely grouped into three broad categories based on interviews and survey data. These categories comprise those more successful *hurudza* (rich peasants) who are already accumulating from below, followed by worker-peasants who are involved in both farming and wage labour. The last category

Table 1 Socio-Economic Differentiation of the Newly Resettled Farmers.

	Rich Peasants	Worker-Peasants	Rural Proletariat
Percentage (%) of surveyed households	5	84	11
Place of origin	Gokwe Sanyati	Gokwe Sanyati Old resettlements Urban areas	Old resettlements Urban areas Occupied farms
Average livestock owned	25 heads of cattle	5 heads of cattle Other small livestock	1 head of cattle Other small livestock
Crop production and average yields	25 tonnes of maize 15 bales of tobacco 20 bales of cotton	5 tonnes of maize 100 kg of small grains 3 bales of cotton	500 kg of maize 50 kg of small grains
Movable property owned	Tractors Ploughs Ox-drawn carts	Ploughs Ox-drawn carts Hoes	Ploughs Hoes
Investments and business ownership	Grocery shops Bottle stores Grinding mills Butcheries	Petty commodity trade	None
Involvement in off-farm activities	None	Wage labour Gold panning	Barter Wage labour Gold panning

Source: Damvuri baseline survey.

comprises of a rural proletariat who have not yet been allocated land and thus socially reproduce themselves through the sale of labour power to the richer peasants. However, it is important to highlight here that these categories are not absolute as the situation is dynamic and likely to change in the long term.

Hurudza (Rich Peasants)

Not everyone who came to Damvuri became a successful farmer or had the means to utilize the land. A small number (5 per cent, according to the Damvuri survey) of new farmers have, however, successfully established themselves as farmers despite the odds being hugely stacked against the newly resettled farmers. This small percentage of the new farmers constitutes a rich peasantry who are already accumulating from below. In Mhondoro Ngezi, a diversity of factors influenced the emergence of people who have come to constitute the *hurudza*. Interviews with informants in this category indicate that some people became successful because they were the first to join the land occupations and hence occupied positions of authority in new authority structures such as the local ZANU PF committees. Such authority structures were instrumental in the way the new farmers could access inputs and other government subsidies such as tractors which were given to farmers under a government-sponsored farm mechanization programme. Moreover, some were rich peasants who already had the means to invest in their newly acquired land. Although they constitute a relatively small percentage of the total population at the former Damvuri conservancy, they have been able to clear their land, build modern-looking houses and own large numbers of livestock. They have also been able to produce relatively large amounts of grain (an average of 20 tonnes) and cash crops such as tobacco and cotton.

Apart from being able to quickly make agricultural investments, such farmers took advantage of business opportunities created by the departure of the former white owner to start retailing businesses. For example, before the onset of land occupations at the Damvuri conservancy in 2000, there was only one farm shop which serviced the approximately 40 farm worker households. In the aftermath of land reform, the shop became too small to cater for the needs of over 185 resettled households. The growth in households has also created new markets for more household goods, agricultural equipment, grinding mills and other services. The biographies below demonstrate how the people who were able to take advantage of these new business opportunities tended to be those who had access to financial resources or those who could utilize their political connections to access government subsidies. In the aftermath of land reform, new business investments made by this small group have contributed to the emergence of a thriving business centre at the former Damvuri conservancy, which has grown from just one farm shop before land reform to three bottle stores, two butcheries and over five grocery shops, two general dealerships and grinding mills. These biographies also highlight the background of the individual farmers in this category and how they have been able to make investments at a time when a large number of the new farmers struggled to establish their farming operations.

Mr Musvusvudzi came from the nearby Mhondoro Ngezi CA in 2000. Before he was resettled at the former Damvuri conservancy, he was a businessman who owned a grocery shop at Manyewe Business Centre in Mhondoro Ngezi:

We came here in 2000, attracted by the prospect of better land for farming and grazing pastures. The soil in the Mhondoro CA was degraded and required a large amount of fertilizers to grow crops. We were running a successful business back in the communal areas and we quickly re-established the business when we came here. Initially, we were not sure about coming here but now we are confident that the situation is permanent. This place has a lot of opportunities; we own a shop and we are growing cotton; we intend to expand both our business and our farming operations. We recently bought a tractor and other agricultural equipment. The soil here is much better for intensive farming, especially for those farmers with better knowledge of agriculture. In terms of improvements, our business is doing well, and we are already building a bigger shop. Our farming will improve with time as we acquire more machinery. Despite the many economic challenges we faced since we came here, the situation is likely to improve with time. (interview with Mr Musvusvudzi at Damvuri on 23/03/2011).

Mr Chitima is one of those who utilized political patronage to invest in his newly acquired land. He came to the former Damvuri conservancy from Sanyati in 2000, and was part of a group of the so-called pioneers who joined the war veterans-led occupation. He was a village chairman and was the secretary of the Committee of Seven, which was responsible for managing the affairs of the land occupiers before the occupation was officialized:

I came here with my wife and five children in 2000 in the early stages of land occupations. Before I came here, I used to own a butchery business in Sanyati. I was also a successful cotton grower with a Master Farmer Certificate. My business collapsed in 1998 due to the difficult economic situation. However, I still owned a head of 40 cattle. I sold half of them in order to invest in a small general dealership back in Sanyati. By the time we came here in 2000, the business was struggling due to inflation. I came here with 20 cows and other small livestock such as goats and sheep. I grow cotton and employ labour, especially during harvest times. I own a butchery business. When we came here, there was no place to buy meat after the white landowner left. I took advantage of the new business opportunity to set up a butcher's shop and want to expand the business in the future. This place offers good farming and business opportunities, especially for those with funds to improve productivity and to start businesses. The only challenge is we cannot access bank loans and the government is under sanctions and thus cannot provide the level of support it used to offer us. Our location close to Kadoma makes it easy for us to transport our produce to the market. Moreover, we also have local markets such as the ZIMPLATS mine where mine workers buy meat and other agricultural produce such as maize, peanuts and livestock. (interview with Mr Chitima at Damvuri on 23/06/2010).

Another farmer in this category is Mr Changara who came to Damvuri from Gokwe in 2000, and was a ZANU PF branch chairman and hence had an influential political role in the newly resettled community:

> I came from Gokwe from the Nembudziya area with other comrades (Cdes) in 2000. I had left my wife and six children behind until we were certain that we had secured land. They later joined us towards the end of 2000 when we were allocated land by the DA. We have a historical connection with this place as our forefathers were evicted from Rhodesdale, which was in this area. I was active in politics and was also a successful cotton farmer with a tractor and a large number of cattle. In Gokwe, I used to market on average 50 bales of cotton and 20 tonnes of maize per year. However, the situation changed, the land became weak, rainfall became patchy, and we were offered bad prices for our produce and inflation made farming useless. We came here in search of better opportunities: land, better roads, water and access to minerals abundant in this area. White colonists confiscated these minerals from our forefathers. I run a successful bottle store and own a large plot both in A1 and A2 areas. I grow cotton and am trying winter wheat and tobacco. I have no problems in accessing inputs, although such inputs are always late, as the government does not have cash to support farmers. However, we will be okay soon. We took our land and we shall reap the benefits. (interview with Mr Changara at Damvuri on 23/07/2010).

These biographies demonstrate that success in establishing oneself was dependent on many factors. First, those who were 'rural entrepreneurs' (Ranger 1985) in the communal areas where they came from had a better chance of quickly re-establishing new farming operations after being resettled because they were able to hire labour. Second, being a member of local authority structures, such as ZANU PF, war veterans association or Ward Development Committee, also enhanced one's chances to access inputs and other government subsidies, which were largely accessed through ZANU PF patronage networks. For example, some people in this category became successful due to their ability to utilize political positions to gain preferential access to agricultural inputs which were generally difficult to access, especially in the early stages of resettlement. Patronage structures thus played an important role in the way those with political positions accumulated assets.

However, these biographies also indicate that agricultural investments and accumulation of assets were not only based on political patronage but also one's financial endowment. Those who had the financial endowment before they were resettled were also able to quickly take advantage of opportunities provided by the land reform as they were able to hire labour to clear the land and to invest in businesses. Others utilized remittances from relatives in the diaspora to make investments on the land and to start retailing businesses. Moreover, given the largely difficult economic environment which confronted the new farmers, people in this category were better placed to hedge against economic and recurrent climatic risks. Access to cheap labour also contributed to the ability of the rich peasants to accumulate assets as poor peasants lacking land and draught power were forced to exchange their labour power in order to access such draught power from the former.

The biographies also highlight that farmers in this category were expanding their agricultural operations by procuring motorized machinery such as tractors, increasing their livestock and hiring labour for both their farming and businesses. Moreover, these farmers tended to link their agricultural investments to their businesses. The ability of people in this category to hire labour and to mechanize their farming operations means that they have made relatively large-scale investments on their land compared to their counterparts in the worker-peasant category. However, it is important to highlight here that 'rural entrepreneurs' in Mhondoro Ngezi did not constitute a fully fledged agrarian bourgeoisie in classic sense. As such, rich peasants remain vulnerable to the ongoing socio-economic environment. Time will tell if the current trajectory of accumulation among this group can be sustained given the prevailing economic challenges and climatic vagaries.

Worker-Peasants

A large number (89 per cent, according to the Damvuri survey) of the newly resettled farmers in Mhondoro Ngezi belong to the worker-peasant category. Worker-peasants reproduce themselves mainly through agriculture and wage labour. Although farmers in this category did not have the financial endowment to make large-scale investments, they have been able to clear part of their newly acquired land, construct houses and acquire some cattle, ploughs and ox-drawn carts. They have generally relied on family labour in order to clear the land and start their farming operations. Those who came from areas near the newly resettled area such as the Mhondoro Ngezi CA generally had better access to extended family networks which were a vital source of labour and agricultural equipment in the period immediately after resettlement. However, for those who came from areas further away such as Gokwe, it was generally difficult to access labour from extended family networks given the logistics involved and they had to make do with whatever labour they had in order to clear the land and set up homes.

An important characteristic of people in this category is that they were largely worker-peasants involved in a wide variety of off-farm income-generating activities, although agriculture remained a key part of their livelihoods. For example, some were regularly employed at the ZIMPLATS mine as wage labourers, others were engaged in gold panning while others were engaged in petty entrepreneurial activities such as trade in household goods sourced through cross-border trade. Within this group were those who had accumulated enough capital through gold panning and wage labour to acquire farming equipment and to hire labour on a seasonal basis. Such people were already accumulating from below. However, others in this group were only able to acquire farming equipment and to clear fields, as they faced challenges in establishing themselves due to the difficult socio-economic environment which obtained after resettlement. The biographies below highlight the dynamics that shaped the way farmers in this category invested in their land and how off-farm activities were a key part of their livelihoods.

Mr Chiriseri came from the old resettlement area of Tyron near Damvuri and was allocated land at Damvuri in 2003; he had this to say:

> I am originally from Gokwe where we were resettled in the 1960s; I was a cotton farmer in Gokwe until the late 1990s when cotton growing became unprofitable due to poor prices and expensive inputs. I moved to Tyron where I was both a farmer and owned a small scale chrome mine. In 2003, I decided to move here in order to leave my old plot to my two sons. I am a gold panner and I am also partly employed as a builder at the ZIMPLATS mine. Since I came here, I acquired four cattle, a scotch cart and a cultivator. I am also thinking of going fulltime in mining since it is profitable. This will give me more income to utilise on my land. (interviewed at Damvuri on 28/09/2010)

Mrs Nhidza is a widow; she came from Chitani in the Mhondoro Ngezi communal area and was allocated land at Damvuri in 2004. She had this to say:

> I am a widow, my husband died in 1999; he used to work in Harare. I was left alone to look after my two sons. We decided to come here 2004 in search of better land and other opportunities. When we arrived here we had cattle and farm equipment to farm but we lacked financial resources to buy seed and fertilizers. However, we were lucky when my two sons were offered employment at the ZIMPLATS mine. My sons have provided me with capital to buy a scotch cart and to build a better looking house; they also supply me with seed and fertilizer every year. My agricultural production has improved as a result; I hire

labour during the planting and harvesting season. I am also involved in selling second clothing which I import from Mozambique; these provide another source of income which I use to improve production at the farm. My sons are now saving money in order to buy a tractor that will help us to expand our farming operations. (interviewed on 29/09/2010)

Mrs Chirango is a widow, who came from the Nemangwe in Gokwe and was allocated land in 2003, three years after the Damvuri conservancy had been resettled. She had this to say:

I came from Gokwe, my husband died in 1995. In Gokwe we used to be successful cotton growers. We made lots of money when cotton used to fetch better prices on the market. I was forced to move here in 2003 because of conflicts with my husband's family. It was difficult to move here, I had to dispose of some of my livestock in order to hire a truck to transport my belongings. It was hard to settle here, we had to clear fields and to buy equipment at a time of economic difficulties and inflation. We are now settled, I have access to better quality land and more space for myself with little interference from my family members. While it has been difficult to establish myself here, we have made achievements. As a single mother I have managed to buy three oxen and build a decent house. We are going to make more progress if the economic situation improves. The advantage of this place is that we are closer to cities and in an area with lots of minerals, water and other natural resources. There are opportunities to work in mines in the area. My son works part-time at the ZIMPLATS mine. I am a cross border trader – I go to South Africa and Botswana to buy household goods for resale. This place is very good, despite the challenges we face, we are no longer congested like in communal areas. (interview at Damvuri on 21/10/2010)

Mr Mutanga is a former farm manager of the Damvuri conservancy. Although he was born in Zimbabwe, his parents came from Zambia. He had this to say:

I am of Zambian origin; however, I was born in Zimbabwe as my father came here during the Federation of Rhodesia and Nyasaland in the 1950s. I have a family with four children. I was a Farm Manager here. Life has changed significantly since I came here. Life at this farm was similar to everywhere across Zimbabwe before independence. As farm workers we had few rights as we relied on our white employer for everything. When the farm was occupied, I played a role in negotiating with war veterans in order to avoid confrontation. I have cleared only part of the land as it has been very difficult to concentrate on farming without support from the government. I am still in the process of clearing more land, as I want to expand my farming operations. I am also involved in gold panning, especially during the dry season. I use the income from gold panning to buy agricultural inputs, pay school fees and buy food for my family in times of droughts. This place has a lot of potential, the only challenge we face here is access to inputs and government support. We hope the government can provide support in the long term. (interview with Mutanga Damvuri on 04/06/2010)

These biographies indicate that people in this category have invested in their land despite the challenges they faced after resettlement. A fundamental characteristic of people in this category is that they owned limited means to utilize the land when they were resettled. However, such people have taken advantage of new opportunities associated with the new land to acquire livestock, farming inputs, agricultural equipment and to hire seasonal labour. Off-farm livelihoods such as wage labour and gold panning have played an important role in the way people in this category have accumulated assets. This demonstrates the importance of off-farm livelihoods to the way a large number of the new farmers have been able to invest in their land. The importance of agriculture to the livelihoods of farmers in this category is demonstrated by the fact that some income gained from off-farm activities was invested in agricultural activities such as clearing the land, buying agricultural inputs, acquiring livestock and hiring labour. Some of the money earned was also used to address immediate needs such as payment of school fees and procurement of food. Since farmers in this category were generally vulnerable to climatic risks such as droughts, they also tended to use income from non-farm activities to procure food, especially during years of drought. Petty entrepreneurial activities such as cross-border trade provided an additional source of income for some of them.

By the time of fieldwork in 2010, some farmers in this category had only been able to clear part of their land because they had to spend part of their time engaging in other income-generating activities as a way of spreading risks. However, not fully utilizing the land did not necessarily mean that these farmers had failed. Across interviews, the farmers indicated that they intended to expand their agricultural production in future when the economic situation improves. Thus, patterns of agricultural investments might change in future as the new farmers access more help or have the financial resources to invest in their land.

One of the most important aspects of the FTLRP which has received limited attention in literature is how the new farmers conceptualize land reform. Across biographies, the new land was viewed as an asset that provided economic opportunities not only in the present but also in the future. Thus, challenges in utilizing the land which confronted the new farmers at the time of resettlement were viewed as temporary impediments to be overcome in the future. The main reason behind this optimism is that many of the new farmers came from congested and ecologically degraded communal areas where there were limited opportunities beyond farming. For such people, access to new land brought with it new opportunities beyond the farm which were not available where they came from.

Another important factor reflected across biographies is that the new farmers did not necessarily view the benefits of land reform as only about acquiring land to grow crops, but access to water, pasture, minerals and employment opportunities associated with new land were all viewed as benefits of land reform. Therefore, land reform was conceptualized as a process which could enhance economic opportunities beyond farming. These biographies demonstrate that, although patterns of accumulation and social differentiation have emerged among the new farmers, success and failure are relative concepts requiring an in-depth understanding of the dynamics of livelihoods that have emerged in the aftermath of land reform.

Rural Proletariat

Not everybody who came to Mhondoro Ngezi gained access to land under the FTLRP. Since fast track land reform has been an ongoing process, there remains a group of landless people who are resident at the former Damvuri conservancy. These people constitute a rural proletariat which largely reproduces itself on the sale of labour to rich peasants. In Mhondoro Ngezi, poor peasants comprise of widows, former farm workers and urbanites mainly from the towns of Kadoma and Chegutu. Some of these people had lost their place of employment in farms during the land occupations or lost employment in towns and came to the former conservancy in search of the 'peasant option' (Rutherford 2002). However, by the time of fieldwork in 2010, such people had not yet gained access to land, although some of them had come to Damvuri as far back as 2006. Such people were living with relatives or friends while waiting to negotiate access to land. The biographies below highlight how they have survived in terms of livelihoods.

Mrs Zirati came from Kadoma in 2004 and is a single woman of Malawian origin. Her late husband used to work as a cook for a white farmer near Kwekwe. The husband died in 1998 and she lost her place to stay. She moved to Kadoma to work for an Indian trader as a maid. She, however, lost the job in 2002 and decided to come to the former Damvuri conservancy looking for land:

> I originally come from Malawi, but I have never been to Malawi in my old age. I think we came from Lilongwe with my father who moved to Rhodesia in search of work in the 1960s. I married a Malawian cook and we had three kids. When my husband died, I lost a place to stay and I had to seek accommodation with friends until I got a job as a maid for an Indian family in Kadoma. All my children left for South Africa; they do send me money on a regular basis. I came here because I wanted a place of my own. I stay with a friend who offered me a piece of land to grow my own crops. I am still waiting to get my own land. Since I am a widow with no livestock and equipment, I survive by working for those who are better-off, and they in turn assist me in ploughing my one acre piece of land. I am hoping that my children can send me money to buy livestock and a plough. Life is still hard for me because I don't have equipment and it is difficult to access farming inputs. I thought of leaving this place, but my friends persuaded me to stay. This place is good, especially if one has their own piece of land to build a home and grow crops. (interview with Mrs Zirati at Damvuri on 11/02/2011)

Mr Ndlovu came to Damvuri from Kwekwe where he used to work at the ZISCO Steel Works Company. He lost his job in 2005 and came to live with a relative from the Mhondoro Ngezi CA:

> I used to work as a general hand at ZISCO Steel in Kwekwe. However, I lost my job in 2005 and wanted to get some land. I am married with four children. I decided to come here but have not yet been given land of my own. I stay with a relative, but survive on working for different farmers and also doing menial jobs for other villagers, such as clearing the fields, repairing houses and selling firewood. My son recently got a job at Amble Gold Mine not very far from here. This place is good if I get land of my own things will improve. We were promised by the local ZANU MP that we are going to be given land; we hope they will keep their promise. (interview with Mr Ndhovu at Damvuri on 12/11/2010)

These biographies above highlight that there was a group of people who did not have land of their own but survived by providing wage labour to better-off peasants. The fact that there were people without land but who continued to expect to gain access to land highlights that land reform was viewed by ordinary people as an infinite process. It is important to highlight that landlessness in Mhondoro Ngezi was juxtaposed with the fact that there was relatively large tracts of land belonging to absentee owners. This is because residents of the Mhondoro Ngezi CA acquired land at the former Damvuri conservancy, but remained in the communal area. Thus, distortions in land ownership persist in the aftermath of land reform and are likely to be the source of ongoing struggles over access to land in the near future.

Straddling Livelihoods after Land Reform

A large number (89 per cent) of the new farmers in Mhondoro Ngezi have struggled to utilize the land and are involved in a wide range of income-generating activities since they did not get government support after resettlement. Although such people have made limited investments on their land, it does not mean that they have completely failed. Interviews with informants indicate that access to land brought with it many benefits beyond the farming. These opportunities have played an important role in sustaining those farmers who lacked the means to farm. But what kind of off-farm opportunities were brought about by the land reform in Mhondoro Ngezi, and how have they influenced new livelihoods trajectories? An important aspect to take into consideration when analysing the benefits of the land reform is that they go far beyond getting land to grow crops. Land reform in Mhondoro Ngezi entailed access to diverse livelihood opportunities such as natural resource extraction, hunting, fishing, wage labour and artisanal and small-scale gold mining. These off-farm opportunities have provided a vital source of food and income which sustain a large number of farmers who have struggled to invest in their land. For example, in the aftermath of the land reform, artisanal gold mining has grown exponentially to become one the biggest employers of both rural and urban people. It has also become a major source of income for agricultural investments, especially among the peasantry (Mkodzongi and Spiegel 2018).

In their analyses of livelihoods after land reform in the Masvingo Province, Scoones et al. (2010: 166) have observed that 'livelihoods in Africa are highly diversified and Zimbabwe is no exception'. This is also highlighted by the Mhondoro Ngezi case study. The new land has brought with it greater benefits which were non-existent in communal areas where the majority of land beneficiaries came from. The newly resettled areas are located in an area rich in minerals such as gold, chrome and platinum. Thus, a wide range of mining activities take place across the broader Mhondoro Ngezi area. The area is also located in an area of relatively high ecological potential (ecological Regions II and III, according to rainfall isohyets). The area is watered by four major rivers, which flow westwards (Muzvezve, Munyati, Sebakwe and Mungezi) and provide fresh water for domestic animals and for gardening. Riverine ecosystems are also a source of fresh water fish and other wildlife, which are harvested for own consumption and for sale. The new land has thus brought with it a wide variety of off-farm income opportunities and provided the new farmers with more food options at a time when many of them struggle to invest in their land. Below, I analyse how these off-farm opportunities have influenced livelihood trends.

Natural Resource Extraction and Trade

At the time of its occupation by war veterans in 2000, the Damvuri conservancy had a wide variety of fauna and flora which became accessible to the new farmers after the white farmer left. In the aftermath of land reform, newly resettled farmers were able to harvest wildlife and other natural resources which were in relative abundance in the early stages of land occupations in 2000. Historically, such natural resources were formerly a preserve of the white landowners and foreign tourists who frequented the area during the safari hunting seasons. In the aftermath of the land reform, the trade in game meat became a lucrative business. It was largely a male activity undertaken through informal networks. In the early stages of resettlement, a large number of warthogs and other small game such as impala were snared and hunted with dogs. The meat was sold at the nearby ZIMPLATS mine, and at artisanal gold mining sites near the towns of Kwekwe and Kadoma. The informal meat markets have become a vital source of income for some farmers, although this cannot be sustained in the long term.

The woodlands across the former white-owned farms of Mhondoro Ngezi also provided a rich array of wild plants and timber which were harvested for both domestic consumption and for sale locally and in the nearby towns of Kadoma and Kwekwe. The gathering of wild fruits and plants for sale at informal markets by the roadside was mainly undertaken by women. Wild plants such as *nyii* (brown ivory), *nhengeni* (*Ximenia americana*) and wild mushrooms were gathered and sold by the roadside or transported to Kwekwe and Kadoma where they were sold. The trade in wild plants and fruits provided women with some income which supplemented their agricultural activities. The wide variety of flora in Mhondoro Ngezi was not only exploited for economic gain, but some informants highlighted during the fieldwork how some plant species with medicinal qualities are highly valued and conserved by the new farmers. For example, certain species of *gavakava* (aloe vera) commonly found in the area are harvested to cure livestock diseases such as redwater common during the summer season. Other plants are propagated and harvested to cure ailments such as headaches, stomach pains and fevers. An informant who is a herbalist highlighted during an interview how 'land reform had created access to a wide range of plants, with medicinal qualities which were no longer available in ecologically degraded communal areas' (interview with Chinyama at Damvuri on 23/10/2010).

This highlights that there are certain types of plants that people are compelled to conserve as they provide a vital source of alternative medicine in the absence of healthcare workers and clinics in the new area. The wide-scale utilization of natural resources after land reform in Mhondoro Ngezi has triggered fears of an environmental catastrophe among local authority structures such as chiefs and ward councillors. Although these local authorities are tasked with policing natural resource utilization, they tend not to strictly enforce the statutory laws governing their utilization. There are various reasons for their failure to enforce the laws. First, since chiefs and councillors live among the people, they have a better understanding of the challenges faced by people and why such people end up over exploiting certain natural resources. This is highlighted in an interview with Chief Benhura, who observed,

> I am against people who randomly cut down trees or engage in careless hunting of wild animals. We want to reserve these natural resources for future generations, however we should also understand that rural people have needs that they to address on a daily bases. If those problems are addressed, such as having access to alternative sources of energy or meat, then there will be less pressure on the environment. (interview at Manyewe on 23/09/2011)

The above illustrates that local authorities are aware of the over-exploitation of natural resources after land reform, but are also faced with the dilemma of enforcing laws if there are no alternatives available for ordinary people. Interviews with ordinary people indicate that histories of colonial enclosure of land and natural resources influenced the trajectory of natural resource extraction. For example, some informants highlighted during fieldwork that 'there was nothing wrong with them hunting wild animals as they have been historically barred from hunting while whites could hunt at will' (interview with Mahachi at Damvuri on 26/09/2011). Other informants argued that wild animals such as warthogs destroyed crops and hence, they needed to be culled. They further argued that it was inevitable that after resettlement trees were going to be cut as people needed to clear land to grow crops (interview with Sibanda at Damvuri on 26/09/2011). Thus, the dynamics of natural resource utilization after land reform are complex and require an in-depth understanding of why and how people exploit such resources. Given the fact that off-farm activities such as artisanal gold mining have dramatically increased after the land reform, these are contributing to widespread environmental degradation which poses long-term risks to the livelihoods of newly resettled farmers.

Cross-Border Trade

Another important off-farm activity observed during fieldwork was cross-border trade. Women from the newly resettled areas of Mhondoro Ngezi were engaged in cross-border trade as a way of supplementing family income. A wide variety of goods were imported and sold locally by mostly women traders. These products comprised, inter alia, mobile phones, solar panels, mobile phone solar chargers, TV sets and radios. The availability of mobile phone connectivity at the Damvuri conservancy and the wider area led to an upsurge in the use of mobile phones among the rural farmers. This created a large market for mobile phones and associated gadgets such as solar chargers and solar panels in the newly resettled area since the new farmers are not connected to the electricity grid.

The location of Mhondoro Ngezi in the middle of Zimbabwe close to both road and rail infrastructure meant that it was relatively easy for women from the area to travel across Zimbabwe's borders in order to import a wide variety of household goods for resale. These goods were sold at mine sites such as ZIMPLATS or gold panning sites. Female informants interviewed during the fieldwork highlighted how they regularly travelled to Zambia, South Africa and Botswana where they exported locally made handcrafts and embroidered clothes which were popular in those neighbouring countries and in turn imported goods for sale locally:

We regularly go to Zambia or Botswana to sell locally made handcrafts or hand broidered clothes that are in demand in these countries. We started going to Zambia in 2004 because life here was difficult because of inflation. We sold goods there and in turn we brought back some foreign currency which was in demand in Zimbabwe. We also brought back foodstuffs such as cooking oil which were in short supply in Zimbabwe. When the economy stabilised in 2009 there was a new demand for electrical gadgets such as mobile phones, solar chargers and solar panels. We import these goods and sell them at ZIMPLATS and at many gold panning sites near Kadoma and Kwekwe. (interview with Mai Mahachi at Damvuri on 20/11/2011)

This highlights how women have become actively mobile and engaged in income-generating activities. Moreover, gold panning sites have also created business opportunities for women, especially the provision of catering services to miners who are mostly single and do not have time to cook. An important dynamic observed in Mhondoro Ngezi with regards to women is that they are no longer bonded at family farms reproducing male labour as was historically the case in communal areas. Women are now actively mobile, travelling across borders, exporting and importing products for domestic consumption and for resale. This new mobility of women has a bearing in terms of ownership of assets at household level. Several women interviewed during the fieldwork indicated that they now owned various assets bought from income gained from cross-border trade:

> I now own two cows and three goats which I bought after selling the goods I imported from South Africa. I also contributed money which we used to buy a scotch cart. This year I bought fertilizer as I want to plant tobacco. Cross border trade has helped me to support my family since just sitting at home as a house wife does not pay. (interview with Mai Maruta at Damvuri 14/09/2010)

The role of women after land reform has changed as some women have been able to acquire assets. Unlike before when ownership of livestock such as cattle was a preserve for men, in Mhondoro Ngezi land reform necessitated the ability of women to own livestock and agricultural equipment such as ploughs and scotch carts. Ownership of such assets has empowered women to have leverage over the control of family income and assets. It has also enhanced their ability to have a say in the way land is utilized and leverage over how the proceeds from farming are shared among households. This does not, however, mean patriarchy has completely disappeared; what is argued here is that the land reform has enhanced the socio-economic position of women through improved mobility and ownership of assets.

Mining

Due to the location of Mhondoro Ngezi on the Great Dyke, a geological feature rich in mineral deposits, there is a wide variety of mining activities taking place across the area. These include large-scale platinum group metals (PGM) producers such as the South African-owned ZIMPLATS mine, Chinese-owned ferrochrome mines and widespread artisanal and small-scale gold mining activities undertaken by a socially differentiated group of people. Although illegal, artisanal gold mining, locally known as *chikorokoza*, provides an important source of income for many newly resettled farmers; it is a largely male activity undertaken during the dry season as noted below:

Chikorokoza (is an important part of how we survive here. Farming is still difficult since we don't have inputs and other equipment needed for farming. We normally engage in gold panning during the dry season when we are not working on our farms. We sell the gold to dealers in Kadoma. We normally use the money we earn for paying school fees and buying food. We also buy livestock and agricultural equipment if we make enough money. Land reform allowed us access to gold as these areas were previously difficult to access (interview with Chinyama at Damvuri on 05/08/2010)

According to interviews with the artisanal miners, income gained from gold mining has been vital for acquisition of livestock, procurement of food and payment of school fees for children. Some informants highlighted that although artisanal mining increased after the land reform as many private farms were opened up, ASM gold mining in the Mhondoro Ngezi area predates fast track land reform. Some of the new farmers were involved in artisanal mining way before they were resettled at the former Damvuri conservancy. Such farmers used to periodically visit gold mining sites near the towns of Kadoma and Kwekwe where they would stay for some months and then go back to their communal areas after accumulating some capital:

I have been a gold panner since 1989 when I first travelled from my village in Gokwe South to Kwekwe where a lot of gold is found, although gold panning is risky as one can easily die in accidents or get murdered by criminal gangs. I own over five head of cattle which I bought after selling gold. Since I moved here, it is now much easier to engage in gold panning since I do not have to travel very far to engage in gold panning like before. Besides, the government is now friendly towards *Makorokoza* (gold panners) as land reform and indigenization empowered us to utilize our natural resources. (interview with Chikari at Damvuri on 05/08/2010)

These interviews highlight how *chikorokoza* is an old income-generating activity undertaken by peasant farmers, and that the land reform in Mhondoro Ngezi enhanced access to minerals such as gold that have become a key part of livelihoods of newly resettled farmers. Historically, it was difficult for such farmers to travel across former large-scale commercial farming areas in order to engage in artisanal mining as such areas were enclosed and difficult to access.

Interviews with informants engaged in artisanal gold mining reveal that, although it has become a vital source of income, artisanal mining is a dangerous activity which is underpinned by violence that in many places has led to fatalities. One can either die through accidents after a mine shaft caves in or can be murdered by criminal syndicates (locally known as *mbimbos*) who periodically carry raids on unsuspecting gold miners, demanding gold and cash. These criminal gangs are reported to operate in collusion with the police and other state security agents and thus are difficult to deal with (interview with Jara at Damvuri on 20/09/2011).

Artisanal gold miners also periodically suffer from state violence, as was the case in 2007 when artisanal mining had escalated across the newly resettled areas. The government launched Operation *Chikorokoza Chapera* (Operation Gold Panning Is Over), a violent campaign which led to the forceful eviction of gold panners and confiscation of their gold and equipment. The government claimed the reason for the violent evictions was that the gold panners were destroying the environment and illegally trading in minerals. However, interviews with informants showed that political elites and some criminal elements in the police with interests in controlling artisanal mining influenced the violent eviction of miners. The government's attitude towards artisanal miners has been ambivalent. In the context of Zimbabwe's indigenization policies popularized by the ZANU PF political party, gold panners have been rebranded 'artisanal miners' (*Herald* 28 May 2012), whose activities are contributing to the growth in national gold output and thus the need to legitimize their activities. However, despite the political rhetoric in favour of artisanal miners, the government seems to be reluctant to amend the mining laws in order to legalize artisanal mining. Moreover, the proposed changes to the mining regulations fall short of addressing the illegality of ASM. This is despite the fact that legalization might address some of the challenges faced by miners.

Large-scale mines such as ZIMPLATS have also provided a vital source of income as they employ the new farmers as wage labourers on part-time bases. Key informant interviews indicate that the platinum mine employs a relatively large part of its workforce from local communities:

> ZIMPLATS has brought a lot of development to this area. It provides us with employment. It has repaired roads, schools and clinics in the area. Through land reform, we were resettled close to the mine. Before land reform, we were not able to benefit from our minerals. (interview with Councillor Chitani at Damvuri on 06/08/2010)

This illustrates the importance of mining to the livelihoods of the newly resettled farmers. Interviews with the new farmers indicate that many newly resettled farmers are in one way or another involved in mining, either as artisanal gold miners, wage labourers, or as petty commodity brokers at mine sites in the case of women. Income gained from mining activities is vital for agricultural investments and to cover domestic expenses. Some farmers indicated during the interviews that they use income gained from mining activities to procure agricultural inputs, hire labour to clear fields or to buy livestock, while others use it to procure food and to pay school fees for their children.

The new farmers have also benefited from corporate social responsibility programmes initiated by the ZIMPLATS mining company. For example, the company helped to fund the creation of a women-led brick-moulding cooperative. The cooperative was exclusively awarded a tender to supply bricks for the construction of the mine's staff quarters. The brick-moulding cooperative has created employment for women and strengthened their economic position as they can now contribute to family income. ZIMPLATS has also invested in local infrastructure such as schools, clinics and boreholes. Corporate social responsibility programmes such as the repair of schools and clinics create economic opportunities for local people who are given preference in the supply of raw materials and labour. Access to the benefits of mineral resource extraction is a key feature of land reform in Mhondoro Ngezi which has improved livelihoods. A large number of new farmers who have struggled to kick-start their farming operations have relied on working as wage labourers at mines or as artisanal gold miners to gain some income which has sustained them at a time when farming was not viable. An important point to highlight is that the benefits of mineral resource extraction are inextricably linked to further agricultural investments, as many farmers indicated in interviews that they used income gained from mining to either acquire agricultural equipment or hire labour to clear crop fields.

Conclusion

This chapter has highlighted that there are many factors that have influenced the trajectory of agricultural investments in the aftermath of land reform. While some of the new farmers have been able to utilize fully the land acquired, new business opportunities have been created by the land reform process. A relatively large number of the new farmers are worker-peasants who have invested in part of their land while they straddle livelihoods across a broad range of portfolios such as wage labour, gold panning and cross-border trade. These off-farm activities have influenced accumulation patterns in this group. There remains a rural proletariat who are yet to access land and thus survive by selling their labour power to richer peasants. Such people remain hopeful that they would be able to access land in the long term.

Off-farm livelihood activities have played important roles in providing alternative sources of income for a large proportion of the new farmers. Such activities have enhanced the economic position of women, as income gained from cross-border trade has been used to acquire assets which have given them leverage over the control of household income. Overall, land reform has allowed the new farmers access to a wide range of natural resources which were previously inaccessible. These have provided alternative sources of income which have in turn influenced accumulation patterns among a socially differentiated peasantry.

Chapter 6

'TURNING STRANGERS INTO NEIGHBOURS': SOCIAL ORGANIZATION AND AGENCY AFTER THE LAND REFORMS

The newly resettled farmers in Mhondoro Ngezi faced various challenges which, among other things, required them to organize socially and collectively address them.

Unlike the old resettlement schemes of the 1980s. These newly resettled areas (NRAs) were implemented without prior provision of social infrastructure and services. Moreover, these NRAs were established on former large-scale commercial farms (LSCFs), which historically lacked basic infrastructure such as clinics, schools and shops. In addition, access to the NRAs is generally difficult as most of the former LSCFs were located far from major road networks serviced by public transport. Another compounding factor was that newly resettled farmers came from diverse geographical and ethnic backgrounds, thus were 'strangers' resettled together with limited shared kinship ties. However, the new social environment required them to work collectively to resolve common challenges. According to Dekker and Kinsey (2011: 6), besides living as newly acquainted neighbours, 'the new inhabitants had to solve various problems of collective action together relating to natural resource management, inputs for agricultural production […] and the management of risk and uncertainty'.

The situation which prevailed at the NRAs significantly shaped the trajectory of social organization in the aftermath of resettlement. Thus, the relationships among newly resettled households have been dynamic, influenced also by their heterogeneity based on class, ethnicity and geographical location. Although, the new farmers shared a common objective of gaining access to land, they often competed against each other to access livelihood opportunities associated with new land. Therefore, an understanding of the trajectory of social organization after land reform cannot be based on romantic notions of solidarity among what has been termed the 'land occupation movement' by Moyo and Yeros (2005). Interviews with informants in Mhondoro

Ngezi indicated that at the early stages of the land redistribution exercise, relationships among the newly resettled households were underpinned by geographical and ethnic background of individual farmers. Moreover, since most of the resettled farmers claimed an autochthonic connection with the wider Mhondoro Ngezi area, such claims were often contested and strained social relationships particularly between those from different geographical backgrounds. However, the formation of associational networks within the NRA by strangers despite difficulties which existed had to transcend these ethnic and geographical boundaries.

New People, New Challenges

Farmers resettled under the fast track land reform programme were immediately confronted by a crisis of social services. The programme involved people occupying land under the leadership of war veterans and chiefs with limited government involvement and no pre-settlement support. Such occupations were only formalized at a later stage under the so-called *planning* phase of land reform. However, even the post-2000 planning phase was not accompanied by the provision of social infrastructure, as was the case with earlier land resettlement programmes in the 1980s and early 1990s. Planning and other related cadastral processes were instead state-making processes meant to entrench state authority over NRAs occupied with limited state involvement.

Although the state sought to impose a hegemonic presence in these newly occupied areas, it lacked the necessary resources to provide social infrastructure such as schools, clinics, extension services and farming inputs. The situation was further exacerbated by the fact that the new areas were boycotted by most foreign-funded NGOs as they were deemed 'contested' by the major donors.

In Mhondoro Ngezi, the occupation of the Damvuri conservancy led to the resettlement of 185 households under the A1 Model (villagized). Damvuri conservancy, like other wildlife conservancies, did not employ large numbers of workers unlike commercial farms (LSCFs). As a result, the conservancy had little or no social infrastructure such as schools, clinics and water sources available to cater for the 185 newly resettled households. In the aftermath of land reform such services had to be accessed either from the nearby Mhondoro Ngezi Communal Areas (CA) or old resettlement schemes bordering the former Damvuri conservancy such as Bandawe or Tyron. In their baseline survey of the outcomes of fast track land reform across six districts of Zimbabwe, Moyo et al. observed,

> There are a variety of social constraints affecting newly resettled land
> beneficiaries, the most apparent of which include unavailability of

suitable water for domestic use and lack of sanitation facilities, inadequate health and education facilities and generally poor planning for any investment in social infrastructure. (2009: 146)

At Damvuri, the absence of social infrastructure affected people differently depending on where they originally came from. Those who came from areas further away such as Gokwe and Sanyati were generally more affected. Such people had little or no knowledge of the broader area, particularly its social infrastructure and extension services (health, agriculture, etc.). Moreover, they had left behind the established social networks which could assist them in times of need. The reason for this is geographical. For example, the distance between the Damvuri conservancy and Gokwe (approximately 250 km) made it expensive for people to straddle between the two sites in order to utilize their CA social infrastructure and networks. The situation was however different for new farmers who came from areas adjacent to the conservancy such as the Mhondoro Ngezi CA and the old resettlement schemes. These people, because they had the knowledge of the broader area, could easily access social services and at times utilized their old social networks to access help and support given the close proximity of their places of origin.

The HIV/AIDS pandemic also posed a formidable challenge for the resettled households, many of which were affected either through the death of immediate family members or relatives. Moreover, HIV/AIDS-associated mortality meant that some families lost some productive members, thus undermining household resilience to prevailing socio-economic challenges. The absence of health facilities in the NRAs imposed a burden on the newly resettled households, as they had to cope with the HIV/AIDS pandemic often without government support. The next section discusses the dynamics of social organization post the land reforms.

Social Organization after the Land Reforms

The new farmers at Damvuri were resettled in areas that generally lacked social services. Empirical data from the Damvuri case study and studies undertaken elsewhere (Murisa 2007; Scoones et al. 2010; Dekker and Kinsey 2011) indicate that despite the challenges associated with being resettled during an economic crisis, the new farmers had to overcome their geographical and ethnic differences in order to address the wide socio-economic challenges associated with the new land. The large number of social networks and new institutions that gradually emerged at Damvuri demonstrates the agency and resilience of the newly resettled households.

Agency can be conceptualized as 'the individual's capacity to process social experience and to devise the means of coping with life even under the most extreme forms of coercion and exploitation' (Murisa 2007: 4). According to Long (2001), 'Social actors possess "knowledge ability" and "capacity" to solve problems and learn how to intervene in the flow of social events around them.' Giddens (1984) has also argued that 'agency depends heavily upon the emergence of a network of actors who become enrolled in the project of some other person'. Within the context of the fast track land reform the study of agency is 'concerned with how rural households respond both collectively and individually to the opportunities and constrains that have the potential to alter their way of living' (Murisa 2007: 5). Furthermore, the study of social organization entails 'understanding the social infrastructure, institutions customs and material and non-material relations that either constrain or enable the individual in whatever pursuit they are engaged' (Murisa 2007: 2).

In Mhondoro Ngezi, social organization was initially influenced by competing claims of belonging to the new land, which created discord and animosity among the farmers. For example, ethnicity and geographical background generally influenced the way people made claims over the new land. This also applied to the way individuals contested for leadership positions in local structures of authority such as Village Development Committees (VIDCOs), Ward Development Committees (WADCOs), local council and local ZANU PF structures. During such contests, people tended to generally support candidates with whom they had a shared history, *vematongo* (*matongo* means ruins). For example, those who came from Gokwe tended to support candidates with whom they came to join land occupations at the Damvuri conservancy. This was also the case with those from nearby Mhondoro Ngezi CA. Interviews with informants from both groups indicated that the reason for this was to gain access to scarce government subsidies, while voting for someone you shared kinship ties with enhanced one's chances of accessing such inputs. As one informant put it:

> We support people we know because they are likely to help us when we face problems; strangers have a short memory, you vote them into power and they will not remember your problems once they are in power. (interview with Mpofu at Damvuri on 19/11/2010)

Moreover, these interviews also indicated that in the early stages of land redistribution, there was a tendency of people to label those whom they did not know as 'strangers' or witches. For example, former residents of the Mhondoro Ngezi CA blamed those who came from Gokwe for 'witchcraft' which they claimed was 'common in Gokwe' (interview with Musvusvudzi at

Damvuri on 12/11/2010). Similarly, those from Gokwe accused the former residents of Mhondoro Ngezi CA for being lazy and for 'deploying *zvidoma* (goblins) to steal wealth from others' (interview with Chikomo at Damvuri on 12/11/2010). Through informal conversations with people from various groups, accusations and counter-accusations of witchcraft stemmed from the difficult socio-economic situation which confronted them after resettlement and frequent crop failures associated with droughts. Moreover, since access to farming inputs and other government subsidies was generally difficult, this created competition and animosity among people of diverse ethnic and geo-graphical backgrounds. In general, geographical background and ethnicity played a central role in the way people were socially organized, especially in the early stages of resettlement.

Between 2000 and 2004, the so-called *jambanja* era, communal area networks remained critical for livelihoods security. These networks acted as reservoirs of labour necessary for clearing fields and setting up of new homes. Again, such networks were also critical in the early stages of land occupations when security of tenure at occupied farms could not be guaranteed. Land occupiers often had to utilize their social networks in CAs as a safety net in the event of evictions or when facing food shortages. Historically, communal area social networks are critical in the way rural households can mobilize labour through *nhimbes* (work parties). *Nhimbes* are reciprocal labour arrangements which are based on established social networks, among people who have lived in the same place for a long time and hence have established relationships based on mutual trust (Scoones et al. 2010).

Being resettled among strangers meant that newly resettled households generally lacked 'social capital' which is necessary in times of socio-economic challenges. According to Deng (2010: 2), social capital is 'the bonding and [...] the stock of reciprocal networks of trust'. In the absence of such recip-rocal networks of trust, people who came from areas further away (Gokwe and Sanyati) generally struggled as they had limited recourse to social networks based in their former CAs. These people had to rely on a small network of people who they either knew from the group they came with during the land occupations or new friends in the new place.

However, as new communities emerged, people who were once strangers became neighbours who could be relied on in times of need. New associ-ational networks and institutions, which transcended ethnicity and geo-graphical background, gradually emerged as people cooperated in order to overcome socio-economic challenges that required collective action. Below, an exploration of the dynamics that governed the social organization of the new farmers is provided. This is followed by an analysis of various institutions and associations that have emerged a decade after resettlement.

New People, New Social Networks and Institutions

The newly resettled farmers at the former Damvuri conservancy faced a wide range of social challenges. The little infrastructure available could not cope with the large number of people resettled in the area. For example, the 185 resettled households had to rely on one borehole for water, which regularly broke down. This forced the new farmers to trek approximately five kilometres to the Muzvezve River in search of water (interview with Mai Chitima 23/11/2010). During the rainy season people often drank water from unprotected shallow wells, which exposed them to water-borne diseases such as cholera and bilharzia. Apart from the water challenges, Damvuri had no health facilities. The nearest clinic was five kilometres away at Bandawe towards the Mhondoro Ngezi CA. There was neither a primary nor secondary school and their children had to attend school in dilapidated tobacco barns which had been converted into a primary school while the secondary school children were sent back to 'communal areas to live with relatives in order to attend school' (interview with Bozho at Damvuri on 23/11/2010).

Some informants indicated that the absence of secondary schools at Damvuri helped to perpetuate the marginalization of girls in secondary education. They further expressed how they were uncomfortable with sending their daughters away to study for fear that they might end up being abused or impregnated; instead, they preferred to send boys away to secondary schools. This meant that a disproportionate number of girls were unable to continue beyond primary education. Interviews and informal conversations during fieldwork indicated that although people appreciated the benefits of land reform, the absence of social infrastructure negatively affected them as reflected in selected biographies cited below.

Mrs Makhaya came from Sanyati and arrived at Damvuri in 2000 and she had this to say about the situation after resettlement:

> The agricultural situation is better than where we came from because here there soils are good as land was virgin land. Our yields are better than those in Sanyati if we were to compare the two places. The main challenge here is that we travel about 8 km to the nearest health facilities. We also send our children, especially those at secondary level, to schools in the rural areas at Mhondoro Ngezi CA since there are no secondary schools here. (interviewed at Damvuri on 13/09/2010)

Mr F. Mafamashiza came from Sanyati and was allocated land at Damvuri in 2001. His family had been evicted from the Rhodesdale area and forcibly relocated to Sanyati in 1952:

We have no health facilities since the nearest clinic is 5km away. We also face serious water shortages as there is only one borehole servicing over 8 villages. I live hundred meters from an electricity power line but my home is not connected to electricity. Our local political leadership is corrupt, we are told that the government donates money and inputs but the local councillor diverts them for personal use. (interviewed at Damvuri on 13/09/2010)

Mrs J. Changa came from Manyewe in the Mhondoro Ngezi CA and was allocated land at Damvuri in 2003:

We face serious water shortages here. If the borehole is broken down we fetch water from those with wells but you have to wake up as early as 4am in order to get the water. This makes life very difficult for people like me who are aged 66 years. Our local school is run down; it is not even a school but is more of a fowl run. We wish the councillor could take our grievances to government. (interviewed at Damvuri on 22/11/2010)

The challenges associated with the new land gradually forced 'strangers' into 'neighbours' and a new sense of community emerged. In 2012, over a decade after the FTLRP commenced, a spirit of cooperation and self-reliance had emerged among the new farmers. Although informants decried the absence of government support during interviews, there was a general perception among the new farmers that through cooperation many of the problems they faced could be addressed. As one informant observed, "We were given land by the government let's work together to utilize it" (interview with Jonasi at Damvuri on 27/07/2010).

The new spirit of cooperation and mutual understanding among the farmers has resulted in a wide variety of social organizations and institutions. These range from a local development association focused on mobilizing resources for building infrastructure such as schools, dams and sinking boreholes. Other associational networks such as local farmer groups, burial societies, new churches and microfinance schemes are concerned with addressing social challenges. A detailed analysis of these initiatives is provided below.

Damvuri Development Committee

New farmers settled at Damvuri were faced with a wide variety of challenges after resettlement. These involved, inter alia, the absence of infrastructure, access to markets and establishing new communities from scratch at a time of severe economic challenges. Although new associations and networks have taken time to emerge at Damvuri, they now play a key role in the way the new farmers are socially organized. In his study of social organization in the Zvimba District of Zimbabwe, Murisa (2007: 5) noted that 'rural communities have developed innovative support systems that cushion against vulnerability and that enhance the quality of life. These support systems include social arrangements of reciprocity, compulsory norms of generosity, communal land and work sharing.' In Mhondoro Ngezi, the absence of schools, clinics and clean water at Damvuri eventually led to the formation of a local development committee.

The committee was formed with the aim of co-coordinating local development activities given the absence of local state and NGO development initiatives. Its leadership comprises village heads, VIDCOs, war veterans, local ZANU PF leadership and the ward councillor. The main aim of the association was to spearhead the mobilization of resources in order to build infrastructure such as schools, dams and drilling of boreholes. The committee also acts as a platform for local people to lobby politicians and to voice their grievances to the state. Its activities involve regular meetings where people from all the eight villages are invited to participate. The meetings provide an opportunity for people to discuss problems they face in their respective communities and propose and/or seek solutions. Common problems discussed range from the absence of clean water, dams for irrigation and watering livestock, unemployment, HIV/AIDS, clinics, libraries and connection to the electricity grid. For example, at one meeting I attended, various interest groups highlighted the challenges they faced and their needs: Mrs Mukora, who represents a women's association, had this to say:

> We need boreholes in every village; as women we have to travel for five kilometres in search of water as the only borehole in Village One cannot meet our water needs. We want the government or the local leadership to secure funds for borehole drilling. (recorded at Damvuri on 23/10/ 2010)

Mr Ruhanya, who represented the Damvuri Primary School Development Association, also highlighted the problems they were facing in constructing classrooms since the children were currently attending classes in former tobacco barns:

> We need financial resources to finish building classrooms. The place where our children are attending classes cannot be called a school, but this is just a shade! We want the government and other stakeholders such

as Non-Governmental Organisations to provide us with help. (recorded at Damvuri on 23/10/2010)

Mr Ncube, who represents a HIV/AIDS support group, also highlighted the challenges facing people living with HIV/AIDS in terms of accessing health facilities and support:

> People living with HIV/AIDS here at Damvuri are struggling to survive, there is no clinic, and we face difficulties in accessing information and financial resources to coordinate HIV/AIDS awareness activities. The coordinator needs a bicycle in order to travel to all 8 villages to support HIV/AIDS support groups. (recorded at Damvuri on 23/10/2010)

Last, the head of the committee highlighted how he had approached the local Member of Parliament (MP) and other government ministries to secure funding for local development:

> We understand the challenges we face which have been highlighted by various groups, we are in the process of organising meetings with our local MP to highlight our challenges so that they can take them further along the authority structures. We are also lobbying local mining com-panies to provide us financial resources to repair roads, build dams and sink boreholes. We believe that in the long term our challenges are going to be resolved. (recorded at Damvuri on 23/10/2010)

These recordings highlight some of the challenges faced by the newly resettled farmers and how they are organizing themselves to address them. What was interesting to observe during the meeting was the fact that, although ZANU PF, which plays an important role in the NRA is generally anti-NGOs, many people highlighted the need for NGOs to provide support. Representatives of local authorities highlighted also how they were going to take these problems to higher authorities or how, for example, they were going to engage local mining companies to provide help. What was reflected was that people did not only expect the government to provide help but also NGOs and private companies. However, this is despite the fact that there are hardly any NGOs operating in the area. Moreover, other people emphasized the need for people to pool resources together in order to address some of the problems, such as donating labour and money to build the primary school.

The Damvuri development committee also acts as a bridge between ordinary people and local state structures such as VIDCOs and ward councillors. It also coordinates local initiatives such as mobilizing labour and financial donations from Damvuri residents for the construction of infrastructure such as schools and repairing of boreholes. The association also plays a central role in the way Damvuri farmers leverage development aid from mining companies operating in the area. For example, the committee regularly set meetings with the ZIMPLATS mine in order to secure funds for borehole drilling, dam construction and construction of schools. The way the committee operates highlights an important aspect of social organization of newly resettled farmers. Informal structures such as the Damvuri development committee and formal structures of authority operate hand in hand in their quest to address local developmental needs. For example, VIDCOs and ward councillors who represent local state authorities play an important part in the committee's activities as they lend both legitimacy and access to other state structures, which is required especially given the centrality of state support in the way vital inputs and other services can be accessed. Thus, the boundaries between formal structures of authority and informal networks, which have emerged in the aftermath of land reform, are often blurred. People have ceased to rely only on one form of authority or organization but assume a dynamic role all with the aim of addressing local issues.

Churches

Since its occupation in 2000, a wide variety of churches have emerged at Damvuri. These range from the popular African Apostolic Faith churches, Zionist sects and mainstream churches such as Roman Catholic and Anglican Churches. These churches have played an important role in promoting cohesion among the newly resettled households. For example, through such churches, some people lacking draught power such as widows and the poor can secure such help from church members. Churches such as Apostolic Faith sects have also contributed to the formation of microfinance schemes locally known as *kukandirana mari or raundi* (a rotating fund). These microfinance schemes were especially central in the way some of the new farmers gained income to acquire small livestock, hire labour and to pay for household expenses and even school fees. Some of the schemes have been particularly useful in helping women to mobilize financial resources for them to buy seed and other property, which improves their participation in the rural economy. The biographies below highlight the role of churches in promoting cohesion, the creation of new support networks and safety nets in the aftermath of the land reform programme.

Mrs Chipiro is a single woman who came from the Mhondoro Ngezi CA. She is a member of Chiedza Chavatendi Apostolic Sect, and had this to say about how the church has helped her:

I am a single woman, my husband died in 2003 and I was left to fend for myself. Life was difficult since I did not have any relatives here. My husband left me with three children, without any livestock of our own. It was very difficult for me to fend for my children on my own. I joined the church because I wanted to feel part of a community. I wanted to have people with whom I could share my problems and also worship. People in the church have helped me during the planting season. As a widow, church members set a day aside when they pool all their draught power together and plough my fields. I feel happy that I found a church with very helpful people. Life is not as hard as it used to be before I joined the church. (interviewed at Damvuri on 22/03/2011)

Mr Chapika came from Sanyati and is a senior church deacon involved in the formation of the Mughodhi Apostolic Faith Church at Damvuri:

We came here and these were *mapurazi* (farms) with no churches. Land reform led to the spread of the word of God. In 2002 when I came here we decided to start a church, we needed to bring people who had come from different places to worship the Lord. The church has been a source of support for many people, the poor, those suffering from *mukondombera* (HIV/AIDS). The churches have also contributed to peace and stability here, in the early days people were suspicious of each other, there was politically motivated violence however through churches people are more peaceful and eager to help one another. (interviewed at Damvuri on 22/03/2011)

These biographies highlight the many roles that the churches have played in the NRAs. Since people were suspicious of 'strangers' or 'outsiders' in the early stages of land reform, churches have to a large extent been a source of cohesion as they have promoted the establishment of new social networks, which transcend ethnicity and kinship ties. Churches have thus redefined belonging as some people are now less attached to 'kinship' ties, as church members have become their 'kin'. They have also helped to address spiritual issues, which have confronted the newly resettled households. Those in need of material and emotional support have been able to utilize churches in order to gain access to help in times of need. As a result, a new sense of belonging has crystallized around the church.

In the aftermath of land reform, churches have also come to constitute an important political constituency due to their ability to influence their members during elections. Interviews with informants who belong to various churches indicate that although churches have promoted cohesion among the new farmers, some churches, in particular Apostolic sects, can be politicized during the elections in support of particular political parties. However, during fieldwork most of the churches tended to support community cohesion as they were utilized by the new farmers to address their social challenges.

Political Parties and Local State Structures

Political party membership and local state structures played an important role in the way in which the new farmers were socially organized, especially in the early stages of fast track land reform. During the land occupations, ZANU PF played an important role in the way in which land occupiers were socially organized and how they sought to legitimize their claims over land. ZANU PF membership was also used to fight against potential threats of eviction from occupied farms. It has continued to play an important role in the way access to land is governed. Interviews with informants indicated that during the land occupations it was important to be seen to be a member of ZANU PF. This enhanced one's chances of gaining access to land, inputs and other government subsidies, which were in short supply (interview with Bushu at Damvuri on 23/11/2010).

Resettled farmers therefore utilize ZANU PF networks as a way of negotiating access to patronage networks, which are critical for accessing government services. Moreover, at Damvuri such membership was not only important for accessing land and government help but also enhanced one's opportunity of securing jobs at the nearby ZIMPLATS mine where an unofficial ZANU PF 'quota' forms part of the mine's human resources policy (interview with Chishangwe at Damvuri 20/09/2010). ZANU PF has also been central to the way people who came from diverse ethnic and geographical backgrounds could work together as a new form of belonging crystallized around the land occupations, which were by default associated with ZANU PF membership. Such belonging provided those perceived as 'strangers' to make legitimate claims over land. For example, those who came from far places such as Gokwe and were regarded by those from the nearby communal area of Mhondoro Ngezi as 'strangers' utilized ZANU PF networks as a way of legitimizing their claims over land and building new social networks.

Through ZANU PF, such people, although dismissed as 'strangers', have become influential in local authority structures where they hold positions of authority as village heads or members of VIDCOs and WADCOs. As one informant argued, 'We all fought in the liberation struggle, we belong to ZANU PF, we should get land anywhere in Zimbabwe regardless of our ethnic background' (interview with Bere at Damvuri 07/06/2012).

HIV/AIDS Support Groups

One of the major aspects of fast track land reform, which has received limited attention in literature, is how the large-scale mobility of people associated with the fast track land reforms increased their vulnerability to the HIV/AIDS pandemic. During the land occupations, most men left their communal homes to join war veteran-led land occupations. Since these occupations generally started as protests with no guarantee that they would be sustained, most men left their wives behind as a security precaution. The process sometimes took many months before a land owner was forced off the land; men were therefore separated from their wives for long periods.

The long separation of men from their wives during the land occupations resulted in men engaging in extramarital affairs, hence the high incidences of *kubika mapoto* (cohabiting) or the increase in polygamous relationships. These new relationships often increased the vulnerability of households to HIV/AIDS. At Damvuri and the wider area, HIV/AIDS has become a critical issue as it has affected many households due to various factors. The broader Mhondoro Ngezi area is a predominantly mining area. Historically, mining areas have high HIV/AIDS prevalence than the national average (Moyo et al. 2009). Moreover, Damvuri is located in a transit area linking the Mhondoro Ngezi CA with the mining towns of Kwekwe and Kadoma to the west and Mvuma to east. The large-scale mobility of people in the area makes it difficult to contain the spread of HIV/AIDS as people are constantly moving from one mine to the other. Chapter 5 highlighted how many of the new farmers double up as gold panners and wage labourers at the ZIMPLATS mine as a way of straddling livelihoods. Mine compounds and gold panning sites increase the vulnerability of people to HIV/AIDS. For example, on the fringes of the ZIMPLATS mine is an informal squatter camp called *kumahuswa* (the grasses) which houses prostitutes who have been attracted by the presence of 'business' opportunities.

Casual labourers (who are often local farmers) at the mine regularly engage the services of prostitutes who not only provide them with sex but also accommodation. The mine does not provide housing for casual workers; hence, the squatter camp provides cheap accommodation. Interviews with informants who once worked as wage labourers at the ZIMPLATS mine and had once stayed at *kumahuswa* indicated that the lack of information about the risks of extramarital relationships and prostitution increased their vulnerability to HIV/AIDS and other sexually transmitted infections (STIs). The situation is further worsened by the fact that there are few health facilities around the area. Moreover, there is no HIV/AIDS-focused NGOs operating in the area.

In response to the HIV/AIDS crisis, Damvuri residents initiated an HIV/AIDS support group, which provides information, counselling and psychosocial support to those living with HIV/AIDS. The support group coordinators regularly attend training in what is locally known as 'positive living' in Kadoma. After training, such information about living with HIV/AIDs is shared with their respective local support groups. HIV/AIDS support groups not only play an important role as a source of information about how to access anti-retroviral drugs in the absence of healthcare workers but provide access to antiretroviral treatment (ART). The support group members access their treatment by sending one person to the nearest clinic in Kadoma to collect drugs.

However, support group activities are hampered by lack of transport. The volunteer support group coordinators have to walk across eight villages in order to reach out to their members. During an interview with one coordinator, he highlighted how lack of transport was hampering his ability to coordinate support group activities: 'I need a bicycle in order for me to travel across all villages here at Damvuri; it is difficult to reach out to all those living with HIV/AIDS without transport' (interview with Ncube on 23/07/2010).

Burial Societies

A wide range of new associational relationships have developed at Damvuri. Burial societies are one of the associational relationships that have emerged and play a key role in the way in which people assist each other during bereavement. Traditionally, when there is bereavement in a rural area, people pool resources together to assist the bereaved family with food and cash donations. These reciprocal burial associations are based on established social networks and kinship ties. However, in the context of fast track land reform, these traditional arrangements have undergone some changes. For example, those from areas as far as Gokwe, who lack any association with former communal areas, have been forced to initiate burial societies as a way of dealing with bereavement in the absence of kin and established social networks. Although these burial societies were initially formed by people from Gokwe, they now have a broad membership comprising people from diverse geographical backgrounds.

The emergence of formal burial societies highlights three important dynamics associated with the fast track land reform. First, that those who left established networks in communal areas had to initiate new ones in order to deal with the potential costs of bereavement in the absence of kin and established social relationships. Second, the difficult socio-economic environment has undermined the ability of most families to make contributions during bereavement since they cannot afford such donations. Third, being far away from one's kin as a result of resettlement means that one has limited access to their support in times of need. Formal burial societies, which have emerged after resettlement were initially started by people who came from far areas and hence were unable to utilize kinship networks based in communal areas where they came from. However, interviews with the members of such burial societies indicated that they now have people from diverse geographical backgrounds and ethnicity.

People who came from the nearby Mhondoro Ngezi CA tended to be less involved in new burial societies as they continue to utilize their old links with communal areas which are adjacent to Damvuri. For such people, burials and other traditional rituals and ceremonies still involve their extended families. Moreover, as highlighted in previous chapters, they continue to bury their dead in communal areas where they still feel a strong sense of 'belonging'. An important case in point to demonstrate the dynamics of burials is highlighted below.

Themba Bonzo came to Damvuri from Manyewe in Mhondoro Ngezi in 2002. In 2012 his son was murdered in Bulawayo. During an informal conversation, he explained how his family decided to bury him in the Mhondoro Ngezi CA rather than at the NRA:

> When my son died after being murdered in Bulawayo by thugs, we decided to bury him at our former homestead in Mhondoro close to where my mother is buried. Although nobody lives at the ruins of our former homestead, we thought it did not make sense to bury him here since all people are buried back home in Mhondoro Ngezi. Moreover, we could not have the funeral here because most of our family and relatives are in Mhondoro Communal Area. (interviewed at Damvuri on 30/06/2012)

This indicates that even though new associations have emerged in Damvuri, lineage and kinship ties with communal areas where some beneficiaries of land came from continue to play an important role in the way the newly resettled households are socially organized. Such networks play a central role during funerals and other family gatherings such as *kurova guva* (a ritual that takes place a year after one's death). However, not everyone can utilize their lineage and kinship-based networks, particularly those from areas far from Mhondoro Ngezi, but they tend to utilize new associational networks. However, this does not mean that those who are not burial society members do not participate in local funerals as all community members are expected to participate. The social organization in the aftermath of land reform has thus been influenced by a variety of factors; these include, inter alia, geographical background of the farmers in terms of location of their places of origin in relation to Damvuri. Time is also an important factor as interviews with informants in 2012, a decade after resettlement, indicated. It highlighted that new social networks based on mutual trust, marriage and friendship rather than ethnicity or geographical background had reshaped the way the new farmers are socially organized.

Farmer Cooperatives

One of the major challenges facing the new farmers was the absence of extension services immediately after resettlement. Such services were difficult to access given the fact that the key ministries responsible for providing them such as Agricultural Research and Extension (AREX) Services were underfunded. Moreover, key personnel such as extension officers had been lost in the large brain drain which occurred after 2000. The absence of extension services, especially in the early stages of land reform, had a negative impact on the farming operations of the new farmers. Since such farmers came from diverse agroecological locations, they had to adapt to a new agroecological environment requiring an understanding of local rainfall patterns, soil types and livestock diseases. This affected their cropping patterns and animal husbandry. Problems of establishing new agrarian operations in new environments compelled the farmers to start new farmer associations as a way of sharing risks, equipment, information and support in the absence of official help.

Local farmer associations that emerged at Damvuri played a role in the way people exchanged expertise. For example, some farmers learnt how to use new technologies such as using knapsacks to spray their livestock against tick-borne diseases in the absence of dip tanks. Interviews with the members of farmers' association indicated that they provided a platform for the farmers to share information and expertise. For example, those with better knowledge of the local ecology such as former employees of the Damvuri conservancy helped to orientate their colleagues to the ecological dynamics of the local landscape. As a result, those who were new to the local ecological landscape were able to adjust their cropping patterns to the new environment. Farmers' associations became key sources of information about the availability of inputs and also provided a platform to lobby local politicians in order to access government subsidies (interview with Mutanga at Damvuri on 23/10/2010).

Most of the farmers' associations were started after 2006 as a result of high inflation and shortages of inputs. They were central in the way the farmers accessed inputs and marketed their agricultural produce. Unlike in communal areas where people could easily utilize ox-drawn carts to transport agricultural produce to the market or depot, Damvuri had neither a grain nor cotton marketing depot. Agricultural produce had to be marketed in Kadoma where the nearest depots are located. Although Damvuri is situated relatively close to Kadoma (less than 100 km), transporting farm produce required people to pool resources together in order to hire transport as one cannot use ox-drawn carts. Moreover, those growing tobacco had to hire transport to Harare since the marketing of tobacco is centralized. Transport logistics thus required closer cooperation among the farmers. However, the situation might change in the long term once the marketing facilities of both cotton and tobacco are decentralized.

Moreover, those involved in the production of cash crops such as cotton needed to be part of a farmers' group in order to access credit. As a risk-control measure, cotton companies require that farmers belong to a group before they become a part of the outgrower schemes which enabled access to credit. Thus, the new farmers had to enter into local farmers' associations as a way of accessing credit or as a way of sharing the cost of transporting produce to the market. Interviews with key informants such as AREX officer indicated the new farmers' associations are localized and have limited links to national organizations representing small-scale farmers such as the Zimbabwe Farmers Union (ZFU) (interview with Chikozho at Damvuri on 24/10/2010). However, this did not make them less effective in helping the local farmers to deal with their challenges, especially in accessing inputs. Through interviews and informal conversations with the members of farmers' associations, it emerged that such associations provide a platform for the new farmers to engage with the state in order to access help since local farmers' associations play an influential role during the elections as politicians target them to canvas for support. Thus, the associations use such periods to address their problems and also to lobby politicians for more and secure access to agricultural inputs. For example, local farmers' groups at Damvuri have used their lobbying power to source periodically donations of seed and fertilizer from Peter Haritatos, the local ZANU PF MP (interview with Hungwe at Damvuri on 26/10/2010). Since farmers' cooperatives have among their membership representatives of local authority structures such as war veterans, local ZANU PF leaders and ward councillors, they have the capacity to access state patronage structures which are key to accessing agricultural inputs.

The Mhondoro Ngezi Community Share-Ownership Trust

An important local organization, which emerged in 2011 in the context of Zimbabwe's indigenization policies, is the Mhondoro Ngezi Chegutu and Zvimba Community Share-Ownership Trust (CSOT). It was created with the aim of helping local communities access the benefits of indigenization of the South African-owned ZIMPLATS mining company which operates platinum mines in the area. Despite the controversy associated with its creation, the trust had the effect of amplifying discourses of local ownership of natural resources among the newly resettled farmers. Through conversations with informants at Damvuri, there is a general expectation among the new farmers that the ZIMPLATS mining company should fund local development initiatives as a way of paying back for the extraction of local mineral resources. Although discourses of indigenization and local ownership of resources have been dismissed as a ZANU PF political gimmick, they have become key to the way local people conceptualize solutions to problems they face. In Mhondoro Ngezi, the absence of 'development' after land reform is no longer a problem of the state alone; foreign-owned companies such as ZIMPLATS are also implicated in the way local people continue to be marginalized while the companies are extracting local resources. Thus, local farmers have deployed the indigenization mantra as a way of forcing the company to fund local development initiatives, as the local councillor put it:

> These companies are taking away our resources left to us by our ancestors. They should pay by giving us money so we can address the challenges we face, if they don't we can force them out, the President made it clear that if they do not want to indigenise they should leave our resources. (interview with Councillor Tigere at Damvuri on 21/09/2010)

On a broader level, discourses of indigenization and local ownership of natural resources, which have recently gained some salience in Zimbabwean political discourse, have come to play a key role in the way in which the local communities organize themselves to address their local problems. At the core of such discourses is the fact that the state ceases to be responsible for local development; instead, foreign-owned mining companies are expected to pay for such development projects by investing in local communities. However, such discourses are juxtaposed to the fact that the local CSOT has been reportedly looted by ZANU PF political elites (*Mail and Guardian* Online 24 October 2011). For example, the indigenization of ZIMPLATS was highly contested by local chiefs and elites in government as highlighted in the Government of Zimbabwe-owned *Sunday Mail* newspaper (3 March 2013). Despite this, local people have been able to deploy indigenization discourses as a way of mobilizing resources in order to address local problems. However, the reversal of the indigenization and local empowerment regulations under the Mnangagwa government has undermined the ability of local communities to pressure mining companies to continue funding developmental initiatives. Companies such as ZIMPLATS who were pressured to pay US$10 million into a local community share ownership trust see no reason to continue funding developmental initiatives as the new government has reversed the law which compelled them to do so. Despite these recent developments, the situation at Damvuri illustrates the agency of the newly resettled farmers in terms of their ability to socially organize themselves to deal with a wide variety of challenges that confronted them after resettlement.

Conclusion

This chapter has highlighted that gaining access to land was not the end of the story. Many of the NRAs lacked basic infrastructure such as roads, schools and clinics. The situation was worsened by the fact that farmers who were resettled under the FTLRP received limited government support and they had to address many socio-economic challenges on their own. Thus, the success of the new farmers in the way they organized themselves to deal with the many problems they faced after resettlement largely owes itself to their creativity. An important aspect of social organization after resettlement worth noting is that it was initially influenced by the ethnic and geographical background of land beneficiaries. However, time became an important factor in the way the new social institutions and associational networks emerged as people overcame their differences and cooperated with former 'strangers' in order to deal with local problems.

It is important to highlight that newly formed associational networks have been underpinned by gender, ethnicity and political dynamics. Some organizations have been more inclusive of gender and ethnicity than others. For example, church-based microfinance schemes have a predominantly female membership, while local farmer organizations tend to be dominated by men with very few female members. Local farmers' organizations were largely inclusive of people from diverse ethnic and geographical backgrounds as anybody could join them based on their needs. Other organizations such as burial societies were started by people who came from distant areas such as Gokwe and Sanyati. However, their membership has grown to include people from diverse geographical backgrounds. Other local organizations such as the Mhondoro Ngezi CSOT tended to be influenced by the broader politics of indigenization of local empowerment. Access to their services was influenced by political party membership, class, ethnicity and gender. It should be noted that as much as the benefits of land reform are celebrated, the new farmers have had to deal with many challenges on their own with limited government support. The fact that many farmers have stayed put despite many challenges highlighted reflects their resilience and the importance of land to their livelihood strategies.

Chapter 7

CONCLUSIONS

This book provides a timely contribution to the growing body of literature on the outcomes of Zimbabwe's fast track land reform process, including on the manner in which land was allocated, the distribution of beneficiaries and the emerging trajectory of rural livelihoods. The book utilizes empirical data and ethnographic approaches to elaborate on specific processes of how the land reform has unfolded, and its impact on the livelihoods of peasant farmers who benefited from land redistribution.

Another important aspect of Zimbabwe's land reform highlighted in this book is the way it has retained a localized character. For example, in Mhondoro Ngezi, land reform was an ordered process which was state-led. The state was 'present' and assumed a hegemonic role during the implementation of the FTLRP and in its aftermath. This ordered process allowed people from diverse geographical, class, gender and ethnic backgrounds to access land and other opportunities associated with the new land. This local experience challenges claims of state absence, disorder and chaos during the implementation of the FTLRP which have been popularized by some scholars (Hammar et al. 2003). For example, in Mhondoro Ngezi, local state structures did not collapse and remained in charge of the land reform, and the district administrator (DA) became a modernizing figure who guarded against the collapse of the local state. War veterans were thus forced to work under him rather than undermine the authority of local state structures. This local experience owes to the fact that local bureaucratic structures such as the DA had a long history of implementing resettlement programmes during Zimbabwe's land reforms of the 1980s. Such a bureaucracy continued to play a role in resettlement within the new context of fast track land reform despite the fact that many bureaucratic structures across Zimbabwe had collapsed.

Yet another important reason why there was no disorder during land occupations might be the fact that Mashonaland West Province is home to many ZANU PF high-profile politicians who acquired farms in the province. Such politicians were reluctant to allow the situation to deteriorate into disorder during land occupations as this would have affected their newly acquired properties.

Claims that the land reform only benefited ZANU PF supporters (Zamchiya 2011) do not sufficiently capture the diverse experiences across Zimbabwe's countryside. In Mhondoro Ngezi, ZANU PF membership was 'performed' and instrumentalized by landless peasants as a way of gaining access to land and government subsidies. During land occupations, landless peasants utilized ZANU PF membership in order to access land. However, such people did not necessarily vote ZANU PF during elections as voting returns indicate. This demonstrates the negotiability of political party identities and the way they were utilized by landless people to access land.

Additionally, the geographical location of Mhondoro Ngezi on the Great Dyke, a geological formation that cuts across Zimbabwe and is known to contain precious metals such as platinum group metals and other base metals, provided newly resettled peasant farmers with a wide range of alternative livelihoods which were not available in communal areas where most of them came from. Through land reform, the new farmers gained particularly unique opportunities for employment at mines which are operating in the area. Artisanal gold mining has also become a key livelihood activity, especially during the dry season when people are not farming. The biographies of the farmers highlight the fact that artisanal gold mining and wage labour on the mines, for example, have become important sources of capital which is used to pay for school fees, food, seeds, agricultural equipment and livestock. The importance of this source of capital, which lies outside the realm of state control, shows how livelihoods and accumulation occur through formal and informal resource extraction activities and markets.

Apart from wage labour, and platinum and gold mining, the new area also offered the new farmers opportunities to start businesses. As the economy has been restructured and markets reconfigured, new market opportunities have emerged. This local experience challenges claims of cronyism and elite capture of land by political connected elites which have been popularized in literature on land reform (Zamchiya 2011). This finding also demonstrates that the outcomes of land reform across the variegated Zimbabwean countryside assumed peculiar and localized characteristics, which defy overgeneralization and calls for the analyses of the FTLRP to take into account these diverse experiences.

Theoretically, this book has demonstrated that redistributive land reform can transform the lives of poor peasants by removing distortions in the land ownership structure which allows them access to land and other natural resources which are critical for their social reproduction strategies and livelihoods security. Furthermore, it has demonstrated that the benefits of land reform go beyond gaining access to land in order to farm; off-farm activities such as artisanal gold mining are a key part of rural livelihoods as they provide capital for further agricultural investments. The fact that a large number of worker-peasants who are engaged in off-farm activities utilize income gained from such activities to further agricultural investments demonstrates that off-farm activities are inextricably linked to future agrarian investments. These findings thus challenge theories of 'deagriarianization' which have been popularized by so-called agrarian pessimists (Bryceson et al. 2000; Byres 2004).

The book has further demonstrated that land reform was a process under-pinned by many dynamics which were often localized in character. This means that any analyses of its outcomes must take into account this diversity of experiences. The increase in empirical-based studies (Matondi 2012; Mutopo 2014) and ongoing studies by doctoral students (interviews with Chambati and Mazvi) undertaken across various provinces and agroecological regions is a welcome development that is likely to address challenges associated with single case studies.

Overall, important lessons can be drawn from the Mhondoro Ngezi case study. First, land reform can address historical injustices in the land owner-ship structure by allowing landless peasants to access land and other natural resources formerly enclosed under the previous agrarian structure. However, the process is not without challenges; a large-scale resettlement of people requires the provision of social infrastructure and other support such as farming inputs. Without such support, it is difficult for land beneficiaries to quickly make investments on their land. Second, and this is linked to the first point, the benefits of land reform are long term; their impact is likely to take longer to realize (Kinsey and Binswanger 1993). Third, redistributive land reform has the potential to radicalize poor peasants, to demand their rights and entitlements to land and natural resources previously enclosed under an unjust land ownership structure and socio-economic relations. Fourth, a radical transformation of property rights in favour of peasants, such as the one undertaken in Zimbabwe, is likely to attract an international backlash from global capital, as it is seen as a direct challenge to the neoliberal regime of property rights.

In the aftermath of the land reform, Zimbabwe was confronted by a dif-ficult socio-economic crisis, characterized by sky-rocketing inflation and economic decline. This was exacerbated by the imposition of sanctions by Western countries which made it difficult for the country to borrow from bilateral lenders. Although these sanctions were targeted at certain ZANU PF politicians, including Zimbabwe's late former president, Robert Mugabe, who were accused of violating human rights and rigging elections, they had a negative effect on the country's economy as many Western investors were discouraged from investing in the country. This demonstrates that any country that pursues a radical agenda of agrarian transformation must be prepared for the potential economic challenges that are likely to emerge in the aftermath.

An important point also demonstrated in this book is that a lot of factors must be taken into consideration in any programme that involves a large-scale resettlement of people. While land reform has allowed landless peasants to access land, climate change-induced droughts make rain-reliant agriculture a risky livelihood portfolio. This means that newly resettled farmers must adapt their farming operations to changing climatic conditions as a way of spreading risks associated with recurrent droughts. Given the above, off-farm activities are critical for rural livelihoods security as they can cushion peasant households against environmental shocks. Furthermore, the exploitation and utilization of natural resources which have increased in the aftermath of land reform is not sustainable and is likely to affect the livelihoods of the new farmers in the long term. This is an area beyond the scope of this book, but requires further research.

While there is no doubt that the land reform was redistributive, this did not address the land question wholesale. New questions and struggles over land and natural resources are emerging. These struggles are underpinned by class, gender and ethnicity. Below are the major issues that remain unresolved and require further research as they are beyond the scope of this book.

The issue of multiple farm ownership and low agricultural productivity, especially among the new A2 farmers who acquired large pieces of land but have not been able to fully utilize them, is likely to be a major source of conflict in the near future. This is because, while some people are hoarding land which they are not fully utilizing, there remains many people who are yet to gain access to land. The excess land currently in the hands of a few political elites needs to be targeted for redistribution. This can deepen the process of land reform and agrarian transformation which remains unfinished business. The land audit which is being undertaken by the newly created Land Commission can be a starting point in the process of identifying such land. Moreover, the imposition of a new land tax is likely going to force those hoarding land to give it up; such land can then be redistributed to those in need. However, time will tell if those owning multiple farms are going to comply with the new land taxation laws given their political influence.

The new agrarian structure has triggered new questions centred on agrarian labour relations which require further investigation. The upsurge in tobacco contract farming arrangements, especially among A1 farmers, has led to new accumulation trajectories and social differentiation among the peasantry. Peasants (from both A1 and communal areas) have now become the major supplier of the tobacco. This has created rural employment and contributed to local economic growth. However, the process has been underpinned by a new wave of primitive accumulation largely driven by the exploitation of peasants by global capital through unjust contractual arrangements and manipulation of commodity prices. There is a need for further research to examine the broader dynamics of this new wave of primitive accumulation in terms of how it has unfolded under the new agrarian structure and its impact on agricultural productivity and rural livelihoods.

The position of farm workers and their tenure rights in former LSCF remains unresolved. While some farm workers benefited from the land reform, there remains a large number whose tenure rights in former LSCF remain ambiguous and thus vulnerable to abuse by the new capitalist farmers. Since the former farm workers have remained at labour compounds at redistributed commercial farms, conflicts are emerging with the new capitalist farmers who have sought to perpetuate the unjust labour compound system, which is now being resisted by the farm workers. Given the conflicts that have emerged in these areas, this is an issue that requires government intervention in terms of clarifying the tenure rights of farm workers who have remained at compounds in redistributed A2 farms. Their current precarious tenure arrangements leave them vulnerable to abuse by the new land owners.

Although the land reform allowed women access to land, many women continue to face challenges in exercising their de jure land rights due to patriarchal structures that continue to control access to land in the countryside. For example, rural women are denied access to land by male relatives after the death of their husbands. This is despite the fact that their rights over such land are entrenched in the constitution. Although women's land rights have been further strengthened by statutory instruments (SI 53 of 2014) which now require their names to appear on tenure documents such as offer letters or 99-year leases as joint owners of land with their husbands, much more needs to be done at local level to enforce women's rights over land. For example, customary authorities such as village heads with no authority to allocate land in A1 areas continue to use their cultural authority to deny women access to land even though their rights over land are now entrenched in the constitution. This means that much more needs to be done at the local level to help women exercise their de jure land rights.

The new land tenure regime has been a source of ongoing conflicts across the countryside. These include disputes over boundaries, double allocation of land and politically motivated evictions. There is a need to strengthen tenure rights, especially of vulnerable groups such as women who often face evictions from their land. Moreover, the current tenure documents comprising of offer letters and 99-year leases need to be strengthened as a way of addressing conflicts. Additionally, these leases need to be made bankable as A2 farmers face challenges in raising capital as such tenures are not bankable. The recent formation of the Land Commission whose remit is, inter alia, to address some of the issues raised above is a welcome development.

Another issue related to the one above is that of informal land markets which have emerged after the land reform. Although customary authorities are not legally allowed to sell land, empirical data gathered in central Zimbabwe shows that many chiefs and village heads are illegally selling land, although this is illegal under the new land tenure laws. However, the increase in informal land markets demonstrates that there remains a group of people who did not benefit from the land reform, who are now utilizing informal land markets in order to gain access to land. There is thus a need for the government to address distortions in the landownership structure such as multiple farm ownership. This is likely to free excess land that could be redistributed to those who have not yet gained access to land.

Additionally, the subletting or leasing of land by the new A2 farmers, although illegal until recently, has become widespread as many of the A2 farmers lack the requisite capital to invest in their land. As a result, they have resorted to joint venture arrangements with former white farmers and other foreign capitalists as a way of accessing agricultural finance. While these joint ventures are crucial for agricultural investments post the land reforms, they signal a new wave of land grabbing by foreign capitalists disguised as agricultural investors.

While this book has highlighted the benefits of redistributive land reform in terms of addressing agrarian injustices inherited from colonialism, the recent policy trajectory in favour of liberalizing the agrarian sector and a return to land markets threatens to dispossess peasants and other vulnerable groups of their land and natural resources through land grabs supported by the state. Such land grabs, which are disguised as foreign direct investment, are favoured by a comprador bourgeoisie linked to the ZANU PF party which has promoted investments in land and extractive sectors. The scramble for land and natural resources (Moyo et al. 2019) currently unfolding across Africa is also affecting Zimbabwe, especially in the extractive sector. While the engagement of peasants and other unemployed people in artisanal gold mining must be celebrated as it has addressed rural poverty and unemployment, its long-term impact cannot be ignored. The upsurge in artisanal gold mining in Zimbabwe signifies a new scramble for land and natural resources epitomized by the emergence of a gold commodity frontier-based exploitative labour arrangements. There is a need for further research to investigate how this new wave of land grabbing and the scramble for natural resources will affect peasants and other vulnerable populations who, until recently, had benefited from one of the most redistributive land reforms of the twenty-first century.

BIBLIOGRAPHY

African Institute for Agrarian Studies survey. 2014. *Land Use, Food Security and Agricultural Production Survey*. Harare: AIAS.

AIAS farm worker survey. 2005/2006. African Institute for Agrarian Studies (AIAS), Harare.

Alexander, J. 2003. 'Squatters', Veterans and the State in Zimbabwe. In *Zimbabwe's Unfinished Business: Rethinking State and Nation in the Context of Crises*, ed. A. Hammar, B. Rapfopoulos and S. Jensen. Harare: Weaver Press, pp. 191–241.

    2006. *The Unsettled Land, State making & the Politics of Land in Zimbabwe 1893–2003*. Oxford: James Currey.

Andersen, I. P., P. J. Brinn and B. Nyamwanza. 1993. *Physical Resource Inventory of Communal Lands of Zimbabwe: An Overview*. Natural Resources Institute: NRI Bulletin 60.

Barr, A. 2004. Forging Effective New Communities: The Evolution of Civil Society in Zimbabwean Resettlement Villages. *World Development* 32(10): 1753–66.

Bernstein, H. 2009. V. L. Lenin and A. V. Chayanov: Looking Back, Looking Forward. *Journal of Peasant Studies* 36(1): 55–81.

Berry, R. A., and W. R. Cline. 1979. *Agrarian Structure and Productivity in Developing Countries*. Baltimore, MD: Johns Hopkins University.

Binswanger, P. H., K. Deininger and G. Feder. 1993. Power, Distortions, Revolt and Reform in Agrarian Relations. In *Handbook of Development Economics*, vol. 111, ed. J. Behrman and T. N. Srinivasan. Amsterdam: Elsevier.

Boltvinik, J. 2010. Poverty and Persistence of the Peasantry. Background paper to the international workshop organized by CROP and El Colegio de México. Accessed 18 March 2013 from http://www.crop.org/viewfile.aspx?id=26.

Borras, J. M. S. 2006. The Underlying Assumptions, Theory and Practice of Neoliberal Policies. In *Promised Land, Competing Visions of Agrarian Reform*, ed. P. Rosset, R. Patel and M. Courville. New York: Food First Books.

Bryceson, D., C. Kay and J. Mooij, eds. 2000. *Disappearing Peasantries? Rural Labour in Africa in Africa, Asia and Latin America*. London: Intermediate Technology.

Byres, T. J. 1996. *Capitalism from Above and Capitalism from Below: An Essay in Comparative Political Economy*. London: Macmillan.

    1991. The Agrarian Question and Different Forms of Capitalist Transition: An Essay with Reference to Asia. In *Rural Transformation in Asia*, ed. J. Breman and S. Mundle. Delhi: Oxford University Press, pp. 3–76.

Byres, T. J., ed. 2004. Redistributive Land Reform Today. Special Issue of *Journal of Agrarian Change* 4(1–2).

Chabal, P., and P. J. Daloz. 1999. *Africa Works: Disorder as Political Instrument*. Oxford: James Currey.

Chambati, W. 2011. Restructuring of Agrarian Labour Relations after Fast Track Land Reform in Zimbabwe. *Journal of Peasant Studies* 38(5): 1047–68.

Chambati, W., and G. Magaramombe. 2008. The Abandoned Question: Farm Workers. In *Contested Terrain: Land Reform and Civil Society in Contemporary Zimbabwe*, ed. S. Moyo, K. Helliker and T. Murisa. Pietermaritzburg: S&S, pp. 207–38.

Chang, H. 2009. How to 'Do' a Developmental State: Political, Organizational and Human Resource Requirements for a Developmental State. In *Constructing a Democratic Developmental State in South Africa: Potential and Challenges*, ed. O. Edigheji. Cape Town: HSRC Press, pp. 82–96.

Chaumba, J., I. Scoones and W. Wolmer. 2003. From Jambanja to Planning: The Reassertion of Technocracy in Land Reform in Southeastern Zimbabwe. *Journal of Modern African Studies* 41(4): 533–54. Institute of Development Studies, University of Sussex.

Chimhowu, A., and P. Woodhouse. December 2005. Vernacular Land Markets and the Changing Face of Customary Land Tenure in Africa. *Forum for Development Studies* 32(2): 385–414.

Christiansen, F., and U. Hedetoft. 2004. *The Politics of Multiple Belonging: Ethnicity and Nationalism in Europe and East Asia*. Aldershot: Ashgate.

Commarof, J. L., and J. Commarof. 2009. *Ethnicity, INC*. Chicago, IL: Chicago University Press.

Cousins, B. 2010. What Is a 'Smallholder', Class Analytical Perspectives on Small Scale Farming and Agrarian Reform in South Africa. PLAAS Working Paper No. 16, Institute for Poverty, Land and Agrarian Studies (PLAAS), University of Western Cape.

De Soto, H. 2000. *Mystery of Capital, Why Capitalism Triumphs in the West and Fails Everywhere Else*. New York: Basic Books.

Dekker, M., and B. Kinsey. 2011. Contextualizing Zimbabwe's Land Reform: Long Term Observations from the First Generation. *Journal of Peasant Studies* 38(5): 995–1019.

Deng, L. B. 2010. Social Capital and Civil War: The Dinka Communities in Sudan's Civil War. *African Affairs* 109(435): 231–50.

Dore, D. 2012. Myths, Reality and the Inconvenient Truth about Zimbabwe's Land Resettlement Program, Sokwanele. Accessed 13 November 2012 from http:www.sokwanele.com/files/images/Masvingo settlement.jpg.

Drinkwater, M. 1989. Technical Development and Peasant Impoverishment: Land Use Policy in Zimbabwe's Midlands Province. *Journal of Southern African Studies* 15(2): 287–305.

Ellis, F. 2000. *Rural Livelihoods and Diversity in Developing Countries*. Oxford: Oxford University Press.

Evans, P. B. 2009. Constructing a 21st Century Developmental State: Potentialities and Pitfalls. In *Constructing a Democratic Developmental State in South Africa: Potential and Challenges*, ed. O. Edigheji. Cape Town: HSRC Press, pp. 37–58.

Ferguson, J. 2006. *Global Shadows, Africa and the Neo-liberal World Order*. Durham, NC: Duke University Press.

Fontein, J. 2015. *Remaking Mutirikwi: Landscape, Water and Belonging in Southern Zimbabwe*. London: Boydell & Brewer

Forster, T., and L. Koechlin. 2011. *The Politics of Governance: Power and Agency in the Formation of Political Order in Africa*. Basel: Institute of Social Anthropology.

Genzuk, M. 1999. Tapping into Community Funds of Knowledge. In *Effective Strategies for English Language Acquisition: A Curriculum Guide for the Development of Teachers, Grades Kindergarten through Eight*. Los Angeles: Los Angeles Annenberg Metropolitan Project/ ARCO Foundation.

Gershiere, P., and F. Nyamnjoh. 2000. Capitalism and Autochthony: The Seesaw of Mobility and Belonging. *Public Culture* 12(2): 423–52.

Giddens, A. 1984. *The Constitution of Society: An Outline of the Theory of Structuration.* Cambridge: Polity Press.

Hamersley, M. 1990. *Reading Ethnographic Research: A Critical Guide.* London: Longman.

Hammar, A. 2003. The Making and 'Unmasking' of Local Government in Zimbabwe. In *Zimbabwe's Unfinished Business: Rethinking State and Nation in the Context of Crises*, ed. A. Hammar, B. Rapfopoulos and S. Jensen. Harare: Weaver Press, pp. 191–241.

Hammar, A., B. Rapfopoulos and S. Jensen, eds. 2003. *Zimbabwe's Unfinished Business, Rethinking Land, State and Nation in the Context of Crisis.* Harare: Weaver Press.

Hammar, A., J. McGregor and L. Landau. 2010. Introduction: Displacing Zimbabwe: Crises and Construction in Southern Africa. *Journal of Southern African Studies* 36(2): 263–83.

Hanlon, J., J. Manjengwa and T. Smart. 2012. *Zimbabwe Takes Back Its land.* Sterling, VA: Kumarian Press.

Harison, G. 2001. Peasants, the Agrarian Question and Lenses of Development. *Progress in Development Studies* 1(3): 187–203.

Herbst, J. 1990. *State Politics in Zimbabwe.* Harare: University of Zimbabwe.

James, D. 2006. *Gaining Ground: 'Rights' and 'Property' in South African Land Reform.* Abingdon: Routledge-Cavendish.

Kinsey, B. 1983. Emerging Policy Issues in Zimbabwe's Resettlement Programmes. *Development Policy Review* 1(2): 163–96.

——— 1999. Land Reform, Growth with Equity: Emerging Evidence from Zimbabwe's Resettlement Programme. *Journal of Southern African Studies* 25(2): 173–96.

Kinsey, B. H. 1982. Forever Gained: Resettlement and Land Policy in the Context of National Development in Zimbabwe, Africa. *Journal of the International African Institute* 52(3): 92–113.

Kinsey, B. H., and H. P. Binswanger. 1993. Characteristics and Performance of Settlements Programmes: A Review. *World Development* 21: 1477–94.

Lipton, M. 1977. *Why Poor People Stay Poor: A Study of Urban Bias in World Development.* London: Temple Smith.

Long, N. 2001. The Case for an Actor-Oriented Sociology of Development. In *N. Long: Development Sociology: Actor Perspectives.* London: Routledge, pp. 9–29.

Mamdani, M. 1996. *Citizen and Subject, Contemporary Africa and the Legacy of Late Colonialism.* New Jersey: Princeton University Press.

——— 2008. Lessons of Zimbabwe. *London Review of Books* [Online] 30(23): 17–21. Accessed 7 April 2011 from http://www.lrb.co.uk/v30/n23/mahmood-mamdani/lessons-of-zimbabwe.

Matondi, P. 2008. *The Question of Tenure and Land Rights in Resettled Areas in Mazowe District of Zimbabwe.* Harare: Centre for Rural Development.

——— 2012. *Zimbabwe's Fast Track Land Reform.* London: Zed Books.

McMichael, P. 2006. Feeding the World: Agriculture, Development and Ecology. In *The Socialist Register 2007*, ed. L. Panitch and C. Leys. London: Merlin Press, pp. 170–94.

Merdard, J. F. 1982. The Underdevelopment State in Tropical Africa, Political Clientelism or neo-patrimonialism? In *Private Patronage and Public Power: Political Clientelism in the Modern State*, ed. C. Clapham. London: Francis Pinter.

Mkodzongi, G. 2013. New People, New Land, New Livelihoods: A Micro-Study of Zimbabwe's Fast Track land Reform. *Agrarian South: Journal of Political Economy* 2(3):1–22.

———. 2016. "I Am a Paramount Chief, This Land Belongs to My Ancestors": The Reconfiguration of Rural Authority after Zimbabwe's Land Reforms. *Review of African political economy* 43(sup1): 99–114.

Mkodzongi, G., and S. Spiegel. 2018. Artisanal Gold Mining and Farming: Livelihood Linkages and Labour Dynamics after Land Reforms in Zimbabwe. *Journal of Development Studies* 10: 1–17.

Moore, D. 2005. *Suffering for Territory: Race, Place, and Power in Zimbabwe*. Durham, NC: Duke University Press.

Moser, O. N. 1996. *Confronting Crises: A Comparative Study of Household Responses to Poverty and Vulnerability in Four Poor Urban Areas*. Environmental Sustainable Development Studies Series No. 8. Washington, DC: World Bank.

Moyo, S. 1994. *Economic Nationalism and Land Reform in Zimbabwe*. Harare: Sapes Books.

———. 2000. *Land Reform under Structural Adjustment in Zimbabwe: Land Use Change in Mashonaland Provinces*. Uppsala: Nordic Africa Institute.

———. 2011a. Land Concentration and accumulation after Redistributive Reform in Post Settler Zimbabwe. *Review of African Political Economy* 38(128): 257–76.

———. 2011b. Changing Agrarian Relations after Redistributive Land Reform in Zimbabwe. *Journal of Peasant Studies* 38(5): 907–34.

———. 2011c. Three Decades of Agrarian Reform in Zimbabwe. *Journal of Peasant Studies* 38 (3): 493–531.

Moyo, S., B. Rutherford and D. Amanor-Wilks. 2000. Land Reform and Changing Social Relations for Farm Workers in Zimbabwe. *Review of African Political Economy* 27(84): 181–202.

Moyo, S., P. Jha, and P. Yeros. 2019. *Reclaiming Africa*. London: Springer.

Moyo, S., and P. Yeros. 2005. Land Occupations and Land Reform in Zimbabwe: Towards the National Democratic Revolution. In *Reclaiming the Land: The Resurgence of Rural Movements in Africa, Asia and Latin America*, ed. S. Moyo and P. Yeros. London: Zed Books, pp. 165–208.

Moyo, S., and P. Yeros. 2007. The Radicalised State: Zimbabwe's Interrupted Revolution. *Review of African Political Economy* 34(111): 103–21.

Moyo, S., W. Chambati, T. Murisa, D. Siziba, C. Dangwa, K. Mujeyi and N. Nyoni. 2009. *Fast Track Land Reform Baseline Survey in Zimbabwe: Trends and Tendencies 2005/06*. Harare: African Institute for Agrarian Studies (AIAS).

Mujere, J. 2011. Land, Graves and Belonging: Land Reform and the Politics of Belonging in Newly Resettled Farms in Gutu, 2000–2009. *Journal of Peasant Studies* 38(5): 1123–44.

Munro, A. W. 1998. *The Moral Economy of the State: Conservation, Community Development and State Making in Zimbabwe*. Athens, OH: University Centre for International Studies.

Murisa, T. 2007. *Social Organisation and Agency in the Newly Resettled Areas of Zimbabwe*. Harare: African Institute for Agrarian Studies (AIAS).

———. 2011. Local Framer Groups and Collective Action within Fast Track Land Reform in Zimbabwe. *Journal of Peasant Studies* 38 (5): 1145–66.

Mutopo, P. 2011. Women's Struggles to Access and Control Land and Livelihoods after Land Reform in Mwenezi District. *Journal of Peasant Studies* 38(5): 1021–46.

2014. *Women, Mobility and Rural Livelihoods in Zimbabwe: Experiences of Fast Track Land Reform.* Leiden: Brill.

Neocosmos, M. 1993. *The Agrarian Question in Southern Africa and 'Accumulation from Below'.* Uppsala: Nordic Africa Institute.

Nyambara, P. 2001. The Closing Frontier: Agrarian Change, Immigrants and the Squatter Menace in Gokwe, 1980–1990s. *Journal of Agrarian Change* 1(4): 534–49.

2005. 'That Place Was Wonderful': African Tenants on Rhodesdale Estate, Colonial Zimbabwe, c. 1900–1952. *International Journal of African Historical Studies* 38(2): 267–99.

Platteau, J. P. 2000. Does Africa Need Land Reform? In *Evolving Land Rights, Policy and Tenure in Africa*, ed. C. Toulmin and J. F. Quan. London: International Institute for Environment and Development (IIED), pp. 51–74.

Ranger, T. 1985. *Peasant Consciousness and Guerrilla War in Zimbabwe.* Oxford: James Currey.

Richardson, C. 2005. The Loss of Property Rights and the Collapse of Zimbabwe. *CATO Journal* 25 (fall 2005). Accessed April 2011 from www.cato.org/pubs/journal/cj25n3/cj25n3-12.pdf.

Richardson, C. J. 2004. *The Collapse of Zimbabwe in the Wake of 2000–2003 Land Reforms.* New York: Mellen Press.

Robertson. 2011. A Macro-Economic Policy Framework for Economic Stabilization in Zimbabwe. In *Picking up the Pieces*, ed. Hany Besida. New York: Palgrave Macmillan, pp. 83–105.

Rosset, P., R. Patel and M. Courville, eds. 2006. *Promised Land: Competing Visions of Agrarian Reform.* New York: Food First Books.

Rukuni, M. 2012. Land, the Environment, the Constitution, and the Advancement of Zimbabwean Society. Accessed 18 December 2012 from http://www.sokwanele.com/thisiszimbabwe/5495/15122012.

Rutherford, B. 1997. Another Side to Rural Zimbabwe: Social Constructs and Administration of Rural Farm Workers in Urungwe District of Zimbabwe, 1940s. *Journal of Southern African Studies* 23(1): 107–26.

2001. *Working on the Margins: Black Workers, White Farmers in Post Colonial Zimbabwe.* Harare: Weaver Press.

2002. *Commercial Farm Workers and the Politics of (Dis) Placement in Zimbabwe: Colonialism, Liberation and Democracy. Journal of Agrarian Change* 1: 626–51.

2003. Belonging to the Farm(er): Farm Workers, Farmers and the Shifting Politics of Citizenship. In *Zimbabwe's Unfinished Business: Rethinking State and Nation in the Context of Crises*, ed. A. Hammar, B. Rapfopoulos and S. Jensen. Harare: Weaver Press, pp. 191–241.

Sadomba, W. 2008. War Veterans in Zimbabwe: Complexities of a Liberation Movement in an African Post Colonial Settler Society. PhD thesis. Wageningen University, Netherlands.

Scarnecchia, T. 2006. The Fascist Cycle in Zimbabwe. *Journal of Southern African Studies* 32(2): 221–37.

Scarnecchia, T., et al. 2008. Response to Lessens of Zimbabwe. Assessed December 2008 from http:/www.lrb.co.uk/v31, n01/letters.html.

Scoones, I., N. Marongwe, B. Mavedzenge, J. Mahenene, F. Murimbarimba and C. Sukume. 2010. *Zimbabwe's Land Reform: Myths and Realities.* Oxford: James Currey.

2012. Livelihoods after Land Reform in Zimbabwe: Understanding Processes of Rural Differentiation. *Journal of Agrarian Change* 12 (4): 503–27.

Scott, C. J. 1998. Seeing Like a State. New Haven, CT: Yale University Press.

Scott, J. 1986. Everyday Forms of Peasant Resistance. *Journal of Peasant Studies* 13(2): 5–35.

Spierenburg, M. 2004. *Strangers, Spirits, and Land Reforms: Conflicts about Land in Dande, Northern Zimbabwe.* Leiden: Brill.

Tobacco Industry Marketing Board. 2014. Annual Statistical Report 2014, Harare.

Tupy, M. L. 2007. *A Four Step Recovery Plan for Zimbabwe.* Washington, DC: Cato Institute. Accessed 10 March 2012 from http://www.cato.org/pub_display,php?pub_id=8191.

van der Ploeg, J. D. 2008. *The New Peasantries, Struggles for Autonomy and Sustainability in an Era of Empire and Globalization.* London: Earthscan.

2010. The Peasantries of the Twenty First Century: The Commoditisation Debate Revisited. *Journal of Peasant Studies* 37(1): 1–30.

Verbrugge, B., and S. Geenen. 2018. The Gold Commodity Frontier: A Fresh Perspective on Change and Diversity in the Global Gold Mining Economy. The Extractive Industries and Society.

Worby, E. 1995. What Does Agrarian Wage Labour Signify? Cotton Commoditisation and Social Form in Gokwe, Zimbabwe. *Journal of Peasant Studies* 23(1): 1–29.

2003. The End of Modernity in Zimbabwe? Passages from Development to Sovereignty. In *Zimbabwe's Unfinished Business: Rethinking Land, State and Nation in the Context of Crisis,* ed. A. Hammar, B. Raftopoulos and S. Jensen. Harare: Weaver Press, pp. 49–81.

Zamchiya, P. 2011. A Synopsis of Land and Agrarian Change in Chipinge District, Zimbabwe. *Journal of Peasant Studies* 38(5): 1093–122.

Archival Files

National Archives of Zimbabwe, Delineation Report Gatooma: file S2929/4/1.

Newspaper Articles

Bell, A. 2012. Farmers Warn That Zim Agriculture Is in 'Major Crisis'. Accessed 20 March 2012 from http://www.swradioafrica.com.

Chinhoyi Bureau. 2012. Locals Urged to Form Conglomerates. *The Herald Online.* Accessed 25 January 2012 from http://66.135.59.88/index.php?option=com_content&view=articl e&id=32283:locals-urged-to-form-conglomerates&catid=38:local-news&Itemid=131.

Isaacs, D. 2010. Zimbabwe's New Farmers Defend Their Gain. Accessed 13 April 2010 from http://news.bbc.co.uk/go/pr/fr/-/2/africa/8617684.stm.

Kachere, P. 2012. Mhondoro Community Share Trust Chief's Bitter. *The Sunday Mail.* Accessed 7 April 2012 from http://www.sundaymail.co.zw/index.php?option=com_content&view=article&id=28037:mhondoro-community-share-trust-chiefs-bitter&catid=46:crime-a-courts&Itemid=138.

Masekesa, C. 2012. War Vets Sale Firewood. Accessed 18 March 2013 from http://www.thezimbabwean.co.uk.

Moyo, J. 2013. Cheap Attempts to Scuttle Indigenisation. *The Sunday Mail,* Harare: Zimpapers.

Moyo, J. 2011. Zimbabwe Politicians Scramble for Trusts Control. *Mail and Guardian* Online. Accessed October 2011 from http://mg.co.za/article/2011-10-24-zim-politicians-scramble-for-trust-control.

Mutenga, T. 2011. Land Reform Erodes Property Rights. Accessed 22 March 2013 from http://www.financialgazette.co.zw.
Smith, D. 2010. Mugabe and Allies Own 40% of Land Seized from White Farmers. *Guardian.* Accessed 31 December 2012 from http://www.guardian.co.uk/world/2010/nov/30/zimbabwe-mugabe-white-farmers.
The Herald Newspaper. 2012. Gold Panning to Be Legalized. Accessed 19 March 2013 from http://www.herald.co.zw/index.php?option=com_content&view=article=article&id=42139:gold-panning-likely-to-be-legalised&catid=38:local-news&itemid=131#. uugtfowaySM.
———. 2016. Fast Track Land Reform Over. Accessed 21 October 2016 from http://www.herald.co.zw/fast-track-land-reform-over-mombeshora/.
Saxon, T. 2011. No Farming Implements. Accessed 18 March 2013 from http://www.thezimbabwean.co.uk.
Zindoga, T. 2011. Mhondoro's Not so Platinum Side. Accessed 19 March 2013 from http://www.herald.co.zw/index.php?id=11049:mhondoros-not-so-platinum-side.

List of Interviews

Arther Manaka interviewed on 12/02/2010.
Banda, P. interviewed at Damvuri on 03/02/2011.
Bere interviewed at Damvuri on 07/06/2012.
Bozho T. interviewed at Damvuri on 30/06/2012.
Chambati, W. interviewed in Harare on 13/01/2013.
Changa, J. interviewed at Damvuri on 22/11/2010.
Changara interviewed in Harare on 13/11/2011.
Changi, C. interviewed at Damvuri on 18/06/2010.
Chapika interviewed at Damvuri on 22/03/2011.
Chari, C. interviewed at Damvuri on 23/11/2010.
Chief Benhura interviewed at Damvuri on 13/09/2010.
Chief Nyika interviewed at Damvuri on 25/11/2011.
Chigumira, E. interviewed in Harare on 14/01/2013.
Chimuti interviewed at Damvuri on 23/10/2010.
Chiwaro interviewed at Damvuri 23/10/2011.
Chikava, G. interviewed at Damvuri on 13/10/2010.
Chioso, F. interviewed at Damvuri on 22/04/2011.
Chipango, S. interviewed at Damvuri on 26/09/2010.
Chipiro interviewed at Damvuri on 22/03/2011.
Chivanga, S. interviewed at Damvuri on 12/11/2010.
Chiriseri interviewed at Damvuri on 28/09/2010.
Garikai, F. interviewed at Damvuri on 22/11/2011.
Gora, L. interviewed on 13/06/2010.
Gotorai, Z. interviewed at Damvuri on 12/11/2010.
Haritatos, P. interviewed in Zvimba North on 25/08/2012.
James, G. interviewed in Harare on 14/10/2012.
Jeche, P. interviewed at Damvuri on 13/06/2010.
Jonasi interviewed at Damvuri on 27/07/2010.
Lozane, E. interviewed at Damvuri on 22/11/2010.
Lozane, P. interviewed at Damvuri on 22/11/2010.

Mabheka, S. interviewed at Damvuri on 12/03/2011.
Mabheka, S. interviewed at Damvuri on 23/06/2010.
Mabheka interviewed at Damvuri on 23/09/2010.
Mutanga interviewed at Damvuri on 23/09/2010.
Madheu interviewed at Damvuri on 24/10/2010.
Mangwiro interviewed at Damvuri on 17/06/2010.
Machikiche interviewed at Damvuri on 21/06/2010.
Machikiche, A. interviewed at Damvuri on 26/06/2010.
Madhe, J. interviewed at Damvuri on 23/10/2010.
Mafamashizha, A. interviewed at Damvuri on 24/10/2010.
Mafamashizha, interviewed at Damvuri on 13/09/2010.
Makaya interviewed at Damvuri on 13/09/2010.
Manjoro interviewed at Damvuri on 20/09/2014.
Mai Chitima interviewed at Damvuri on 23/11/2010.
Manaka, A. interviewed at Damvuri on 12/02/2011.
Mangwiro interviewed at Damvuri on 12/09/2011.
Mangwiro, T. interviewed at Damvuri on 17/06/2010.
Mr Chikonzi interviewed at Damvuri on 20/11/2010.
Mr Changara interviewed at Damvuri on 23/07/2010.
Mr Chitiki interviewed at Damvuri on 24/07/2010.
Mr Chitima interviewed at Damvuri on 23/06/2010.
Mr Musvusvudzi interviewed at Damvuri on 23/03/2011.
Mr Mutanga interviewed at Damvuri on 4/06/2010.
Mr Ndhovhu interviewed at Damvuri on 12/11/2010.
Mrs Chirango interviewed at Damvuri on 21/10/2010.
Mrs Mpofu interviewed at Damvuri on 14/07/2010.
Mrs Mukaro interviewed at Damvuri on 20/10/2010.
Mrs Zirati interviewed at Damvuri on 11/02/2011.
Mhande interviewed at Damvuri on 24/10/2010.
Mhuru interviewed at Damvuri 28/10/2011.
Mujakachi, F. interviewed at Damvuri on 06/02/2011.
Mujeki, T. interviewed at Damvuri on 08/11/2010.
Munemo, A. interviewed at Damvuri on 10/10/2010.
Munyonga interviewed at Damvuri on 23/06/2012.
Murape interviewed at Damvuri on 20/01/2011.
Muremo, P. interviewed at Damvuri on 10/10/2010.
Murira, P. interviewed at Damvuri on 23/12/2010.
Musvusvudzi, P. interviewed at Damvuri 12/09/2011.
Musvusvudzi, P. interviewed at Damvuri on 24/09/2010.
Mutaka, P. interviewed at Damvuri on 22/11/2011.
Mutanga interviewed at Damvuri on 07/08/2010.
Mutanga, L. interviewed at Damvuri on 23/09/2010.
Mutanga, W. interviewed at Damvuri on 23/06/2010.
Muteka interviewed at Damvuri on 27/11/2010.
Ncube interviewed at Damvuri on 23/07/2010.
Ndhlovu, E. interviewed at Damvuri on 26/03/2011.
Ndlovu, C. interviewed at Damvuri on 22/11/2010.
Nhidza. interviewed at Damvuri on 29/09/2010.

Nyati. F. interviewed at Damvuri on 10/06/2010.
Phiri, B. interviewed at Damvuri on 26/11/2010.
Shangari, S. interviewed at Damvuri on 15/10/2011.
Sibanda, S. interviewed at Damvuri on 19/11/2010.
Sibanda interviewed at Damvuri on 23/10/2010.
Tembo interviewed at Damvuri on 04/02/2011.
Tichafa, M. interviewed at Damvuri on 12/09/2010.
Tigere interviewed at Damvuri on 21/09/2010.
Thimba interviewed at Damvuri on 12/02/2011
War Veteran leader interviewed at Damvuri on 21/08/2010.
VIDCO chairman interviewed on 15/05/2011.

List of Meetings

Recorded at ZANU PF meeting held at Damvuri on 23/7/2010.
Mrs Mukora's contribution to the Damvuri Development Association meeting held on 23/10/2010.
Mr Ruhanya's contribution to the Damvuri Development Association meeting held at Damvuri on 23/10/2010.
Mr Ncube's contribution to the Damvuri Development Association meeting held at Damvuri on 23/10/2010.

INDEX

Page numbers in bold indicate citation to tables and those in bold italics, to figures.

www.ingramcontent.com/pod-product-compliance
Lightning Source LLC
Chambersburg PA
CBHW020004290326
41935CB00007B/298